Meet the Dalmatian

D0337440

The Dalmatian is classified as a Non Sporting dog.

It is theorized that the first spotted dog was seen in a place called Dalmatia in southern Yugoslavia.

The Dalmatian has spots because historically, as a fire wagon and carriage escort, it was impor- tant for other travelers to be able to see the Dal coming.

There are two different types of Dalmatians: white colored with black spots and white colored with liver-colored spots.

Genetically, the Dal is a black or liver-colored dog with a gene for covering the black or liver with white.

Dals are known for their instinct to investigate and are great watch dogs. When you have visitors over to your house, you can expect your Dal to give them a cautious once-over instead of wagging his tail vigorously.

Dalma... ...ous.

One o... ...the Dalma-tian is the ability to "smile." When Dalmatians get flustered or excited, they draw up their lips and pull back the edges of their mouths, ex-posing almost every tooth in the same movement that humans would use to smile.

An active adult Dalma-tian can eat 6 to 9 cups of kibble per day.

Dalmatians need plenty of exercise. They make great jogging or biking partners!

Dal hair naturally sheds and the spiky white hairs cling to materials.

Dalmatians do not require much groom-ing.

Dalmatians became glamorous stars after the 1960 release of the Walt Disney production, *101 Dalmatians.*

Consulting Editor
IAN DUNBAR PH.D., MRCVS

Featuring Photographs by
WINTER CHURCHILL
PHOTOGRAPHY

Howell Book House

An Imprint of Macmillan General Reference USA
A Pearson Education Macmillan Company
1633 Broadway
New York, NY 10019

Macmillan Publishing books may be purchased for
business or sales promotional use. For information
please write: Special Markets Department,
Macmillan Publishing USA, 1633 Broadway,
New York, NY 10019.

Copyright © 1999 by Howell Book House
Copyright © 1999 all photography by Winter
Churchill Photography unless otherwise noted.

The Essential Dalmatian is an abridged edition of
*The Dalmatian: An Owner's Guide to a Happy
Healthy Pet,* first published in 1995.

All rights reserved. No part of this book may be
reproduced or transmitted in any form or by any
means, electronic or mechanical, including photo-
copying, recording, or by an information storage
and retrieval system, without permission in writing
from the Publisher.

MACMILLAN is a registered trademark of Pearson
Education.

Library of Congress Cataloging-in-Publication
Data
        The essential dalmatian / consulting
editor, Ian Dunbar; featuring photographs by
Kerrin Winter and Dale Churchill.
        p.   cm.
    Includes bibliographical references and index.
    ISBN 1-58245-024-2
        Dalmatian dog.   I. Dunbar, Ian.
    SF429.D3E77   1999   98-48816
    636.72—dc21   CIP

Manufactured in the United States of America
10 9 8 7 6 5 4 3 2 1

Series Director: Michele Matrisciani
Production Team: Carrie Allen, Clint Lahnen,
    Carol Sheehan, Dennis Sheehan, Terri Sheehan
Book Design: Paul Costello
Photography: Courtesy of Diana Robinson: *73, 80-81*
    All other photos by Winter Churchill Photo-
    graphy.

ARE YOU READY?!

☐ Have you prepared your home
and your family for your new
pet?

☐ Have you gotten the proper
supplies you'll need to care for
your dog?

☐ Have you found a veterinarian
that you (and your dog) are
comfortable with?

☐ Have you thought about how
you want your dog to behave?

☐ Have you arranged your schedule to accommodate your dog's
needs for exercise and attention?

*No matter what stage you're at with
your dog—still thinking about getting one, or he's already part of the
family—this Essential guide will
provide you with the practical information you need to understand and
care for your canine companion. Of
course you're ready—you have this
book!*

THE ESSENTIAL

Dalmatian

The Dalmatian's Senses

SOUND

Dalmatians carry a gene for deafness. However, the number born totally deaf or deaf in one ear is minimized by selective breeding. When free of this defect, Dals can hear about four times better than we can, and they can hear high-pitched sounds especially well.

SIGHT

Dalmatians can detect movement at a greater distance than we can, but they can't see as well up close. They can also see better in less light, but can't distinguish many colors.

TASTE

Dalmatians have fewer taste buds than we do, so they're likelier to try anything—and usually do, which is why it's important for their owners to monitor their food intake. Dogs are omnivorous, which means they eat meat as well as vegetables.

TOUCH

Dals are social animals and love to be petted, groomed and played with.

SMELL

A Dalmatian's nose is his greatest sensory organ. A dog's sense of smell is so great he can follow a trail that's weeks old, detect odors diluted to one-millionth the concentration we'd need to notice them, even sniff out a person under water!

CHAPTER ONE

Getting to Know Your Dalmatian

1

The inner world of Dalmatians contains wonders around every corner. They are instantly curious about nearly everything and won't hesitate to go see what's up.

The Dalmatian breed standard calls for poise and alertness and a stable and outgoing—yet dignified—temperament. You should understand that this translates into a dog that does not go wagging up to any stranger and lick them up one side and down the other. This means that when a Dalmatian meets strangers, he usually prefers to go up to them at his own pace, investigating fairly thoroughly before becoming the wagging, silly, bouncing friend.

The Dalmatian's amazing capacity for physical activity and endurance seems to be matched by amazing bursts of genius as well. They will test your patience and keep you on your toes, but they are also as devoted as they are smart.

BRED TO JUDGE SAFETY

The Dalmatian was bred to take control of the streets and make

CHARACTERISTICS OF THE DALMATIAN

- Curious about everything
- Alert
- Innate concern for master/family
- People-oriented
- Mischievous
- Quick learners
- Exuberant greeters

judgments on whether things were safe or not for the horses and masters. Although it is no longer common to see a Dalmatian clearing the streets for carriages, the inherent nature of the breed to judge and protect is seen in the way a Dal approaches a new visitor or a new environment. For instance, they are more likely to meet someone by going through the steps of investigation and observation before acting like a wagging fool. Sometimes they are so comprehensive in their investigation that it is

Dalmatians always let their curiosity get the best of them. One of their most innate qualities is the need to investigate.

an enigma to try to figure out what Dals are looking at or smelling.

MISCHIEVOUS AND SMART

Before you get the impression that the Dal's world is all business, duty and doing the right thing, there's something you should know. They're sometimes mischievous and a bit too big for their own britches. The Dal has a large capacity for learning commands quickly—that's the smart part. But once he's got it, the next time you give the command, he'll hear it, remember it, look at you and then decide whether he really wants to

do it or not. Sometimes he will, but often he will not. Certainly mischievous!

Dal's also have a tendency to invent new ways to do naughty things and the capacity to remember and figure out new methods that can drive Dal owners nuts. It can become a contest of wills, which has its hazards: If the Dal gets the idea that persistence and ingenuity will produce a reward (if he "wins" the contest), you have created a relationship where he thinks there are no limits to what he can get if he just applies himself. The owners, on the other hand, may decide that their dog is incredibly knot-headed and does not learn.

Dals are smart, playful and fun-loving companions.

Actually, the dog has learned and believes that he is smarter than his owner, and that he should be able, with enough effort, to get his way in any area he desires.

IF AT FIRST YOUR DAL DOES SUCCEED...

A Dalmatian owner has to be smarter than his or her dog and must be consistent with regard to rules of behavior. This consistency is also required of everyone else in the household, because if the Dal discovers that one person in a three- or four-member household allows him to do a certain thing—say, jump up—and the other household members do not, he will generalize this discovery to the entire human population. Hence, he will try jumping up on guests, visitors and strangers on the street, thinking that one out of three or at least some people will allow him to jump up. The Dalmatian's natural persistence, tenacity and inventiveness could make him a nuisance in the hands of a lazy or unresponsive owner. Like small children, Dals will get your attention, one way or another.

Allowing your Dalmatian to get away with bad behavior (like pawing for attention) once will instill that behavior in him for the rest of his life.

But once they get your attention, they don't always know what to do with it. Sometimes they give the silliest-looking apologetic grin imaginable. One of the curious characteristics of the Dalmatian is its ability to "smile." To some people it looks more like an ear-to-ear silent snarl than a look of glee, and to others it appears to be an embarrassed grin. In any case, when some Dalmatians get mustered, they draw up their lips and pull back the edges of their mouths, exposing almost every tooth in the same movement that humans would use to smile—but they're not laughing.

SMILING DOGS

They look like the fox who just cleaned out the henhouse with no one the wiser, but the smile usually only appears just after they've been discovered in the kitchen with the contents of an entire garbage sack carefully spread all over the floor, or when their master uses a scolding tone of voice, or when they've just found and shredded another roll of bathroom tissue. It's actually a look of supplication ("Don't throw me out of the house! I couldn't help myself, honest!") and it's apparently

a genetic recessive trait. The smiler will lower his head and often slink while displaying the look. Although it appears most frequently when Dals know they've done something that will get them into hot water, it also shows up in isolated cases.

ATTENTION SETS BOUNDARIES

The key to having a good relationship with a Dalmatian is in the amount of attention and affection with which you establish boundaries of behavior. They are eagerly responsive to attention, games, praise and positive strokes. They have a memory like an elephant, however, for coercive, negative or harshly corrective actions. They will respond much more readily to rewards for approximating desired behavior than being forced into the position or pose or posture you wish them to assume.

The difference, for instance, in holding out a reward until they sit versus pushing down on their hindquarters while pulling up on their lead while commanding them to "sit!" lies in two critical areas. They will more readily and consistently respond to a "sit" command

5

Dalmatians are relationship-oriented and love nothing more than spending time with their families.

a person unacquainted with Dals approaches a Dal home and is greeted by a full-grown, adult dog, sometimes impressions can be misleading. There's no question that Dalmatians get excited when someone—even a familiar friend—comes on the property or to the door. They sound the alarm and want to be the first one there to check out the visitor. Proper training will take care of any barking or control problems in this area, but guests who are greeted in this manner, especially people who have heard that Dals are "hyper," could easily confirm what they have heard by the excitement they first see. Hopefully, they will stay long enough to see the exuberant greeting followed by the normal pattern, which usually includes happy acceptance followed by settling back down for a snooze under the dining-room table or in front of the fireplace. But they shouldn't be too surprised to see that when they're ready to leave, the Dal wakes up and treats their departure with similar gusto.

If puppies have been raised in a calm environment with their mothers; if they have been touched, petted and handled regularly by the breeder; if they have been properly vaccinated and wormed; if they

taught through play learning, and they won't start calculating how they can avoid you or avoid sitting, or get back at you for the "pushy" approach to training. No dog is happily responsive to abusive training practices, but the Dalmatian has a peculiarly sharp memory for affronts. They generalize here, too: If they have had a bad experience learning how to sit, they're almost certain to resist other obedience lessons which take on the same manipulative tone.

It is a fact that Dalmatians have excessive energy and are hyper. When have been weaned to a good quality puppy chow; if they were taken from their litter by their new owner no earlier than 7 weeks of age; and if they were introduced to their new home life with kindness, thoughtfulness and sensitivity, then chances are good that you won't see any behavior abnormalities.

UNDERSTAND SHYNESS

If you see behavior that you fear to be shyness within a litter, note that puppies in a whelping box regularly run over one another and try to see if their brothers' and sisters' ears will chew off from five to eight weeks of age. They also establish a pecking order during this period of time. The pecking order demands recognition of who's the biggest and most dominant male or female and who's next and so on. The ones on the bottom of the pecking order are the quieter ones, who cover their ears and get run over the most. They

may go about their business at some distance away from the other puppies, and they may squeal and squirm to get back to their box when you pick them up, but that doesn't necessarily indicate shyness. Shyness is more like having a puppy regard you as a horrible monster even after you've gently picked it up and cuddled it two or three times. (And even this reaction can be related to other causes. For example, as puppies open their eyes, their first reaction to actual visual recognition of your face as you hold them and look at them is often one of startled horror—even though you may have picked them up and calmly snuggled them without incident numerous times before their first real live glimpse.)

The low puppy on the totem pole will not give you an indication of how he will act in your home. In the vast majority of cases, there is a good temperament inside each puppy. It will bloom in response to the love, nurturing and careful discipline provided by the new owner.

CHAPTER TWO

Homecoming

TIME FOR A NEW HOME

You've found a breeder who is willing to refer you to others who own dogs they've produced, or you've asked around and found them on your own. You've learned that the breeding program produces healthy, good-tempered dogs, and the breeder let you look at the litter at 4 to 5 weeks of age. You saw a puppy you

liked and found that she was in an acceptable price range, and you introduced yourself to her by letting her crawl into your sleeve and around your neck, and nibble your ear; you let her do the same with each of your family members. The contract was signed, spay/neuter conditions agreed upon and your fenced yard and house have been set up for a new four-footed family member. Now she's 7 weeks old. At last, it's time to go home!

You have to remember that this is a huge change for the puppy, from an environment of brothers and sisters and mom to a completely new set of sights, smells and sounds, including humans who are ten to twenty times or more larger than they are. Small wonder if they appear cautious or a bit frightened in reaction to their new setting.

LEARNING ABOUT PUPPIES

One of the things to remember about puppies is that they don't do much else than eat and sleep and crawl around looking for another meal for about the first three weeks. The mother provides most of the stimulation in their lives. From about 3 weeks to 5 weeks of age, they begin to notice each other, but they still function mainly in the eat and sleep modes, and play little. From the age of 5 weeks, they start their pecking order and dogdom social education by playing with one another, picking on one another, learning how to get along in a group and learning how to let the others know when they've had enough. It's at this age that the puppies look a lot like the Disney Dalmatians, rolling and frolicking after one another like a barrel of monkeys.

There are a few points to remember about this sequence of litter growth. First, if you get a chance to see a 3- to 5-week-old litter of puppies, and they do nothing but awaken from a drowse and walk around sleepily for two or three minutes and then pile up and go back to sleep again, it's not necessarily a sign of sloth or low I.Q. They are simply eating, sleeping and growing at this stage. Second, because they are actively forming a pecking order and pack social order, size plays an important part in the outward appearance of individual personality when the litter is together. The puppy that's 2 ounces heavier may rule the pack and overshadow the others, and the remaining individuals in the litter may be holding back some of their own personality in deference to the leader.

As noted in the last chapter, one of our Best in Show dogs was an obviously beautiful puppy who stepped aside every time the litter leader—who was himself a very pretty puppy—ran through the room. The puppy we picked didn't blossom with his own personality until he came home with us, but then he became one of the most eager, friendly, tail-wagging show dogs we ever had.

One of the lessons for the novice looking for a pet is that a breeding line with good personality characteristics tends to reproduce those

PUPPY ESSENTIALS

To prepare yourself and your family for your puppy's homecoming, and to be sure your pup has what she needs, you should obtain the following:

Food and Water Bowls: One for each. We recommend stainless steel or heavy crockery—something solid but easy to clean.

Bed and/or Crate Pad: Something soft, washable and big enough for your soon-to-be-adult dog.

Crate: Make housetraining easier and provide a safe, secure den for your dog with a crate—it only looks like a cage to you!

Toys: As much fun to buy as they are for your pup to play with. Don't overwhelm your puppy with too many toys, though, especially the first few days she's home. And be sure to include something hollow you can stuff with goodies, like a Kong.

I.D. Tag: Inscribed with your name and phone number.

Collar: An adjustable buckle collar is best. Remember, your pup's going to grow fast!

Leash: Style is nice, but durability and your comfort while holding it count, too. You can't go wrong with leather for most dogs.

Grooming Supplies: The proper brushes, special shampoo, toenail clippers, a toothbrush and doggy toothpaste.

personality traits. So if you don't see it in the litter box (as in the case of the puppies overshadowed by the "alpha" or "pack leader" litter puppy), it doesn't necessarily mean that an actual absence of zeal exists. The thing to watch for is a defensive puppy who exhibits frightened behavior whenever stimulated by either other puppies or people. This caution does not include the puppy that simply stays beyond the reach of your hand or runs away from a larger puppy; rather, it's the one who is consistently alarmed by and frightened of outside stimulation. You'll rarely find this trait if the breeding line is producing good temperament.

LEARNING FROM THE LITTER

One other consideration is that for the first seven weeks of puppies' lives, they are learning how to form relationships with each other. They're also learning their approach to relationships with other dogs in general. The litter box relationships that naturally blossom amongst terriers are markedly different than those of St. Bernards, Chihuahuas or Dalmatians, but the point is that each puppy—regardless of breed—must undertake this learning at these ages; otherwise, they may be confused about how to interact with other dogs later in their lives. The puppy that is taken from the litter before 7 weeks of age may fear other dogs as an adult. Because this learning stage exists, leave them with their litter for a minimum of seven weeks. If you don't, you may wind up with a dog that bonds wonderfully with humans, but—especially as an adult—displays unacceptable behavior (usually based on fear) in reaction to other dogs.

One final thought on litters through 7 weeks of age: It is almost impossible to set a price on puppies before 7 weeks of age. This is especially true for Dalmatians, because things like nose and eye pigment may be uncertain through 7 weeks of age or more; structural considerations may also be impossible to evaluate before they're ready to be ranked for relative quality in the litter, and the prices will most likely vary according to qualitative distinctions. So if you go to see a litter and fall in love with a particular dog, don't be surprised if the litter owner has a difficult time setting a price on the puppy before 7 or 8 weeks of

IDENTIFY YOUR DOG

It is a terrible thing to think about, but your dog could somehow, someday, get lost or stolen. For safety's sake, every dog should wear a buckle collar with an identification tag. A tag is the first thing a stranger will look for on a lost dog. Inscribe the tag with your dog's name and your name and phone number.

There are two ways to permanently identify your dog. The first is a tattoo, placed on the inside of your dog's thigh. The tattoo should be your social security number or your dog's AKC registration number. The second is a microchip, a rice-sized pellet that is inserted under the dog's skin at the base of the neck, between the shoulder blades. When a scanner is passed over the dog, it will beep, notifying the person that the dog has a chip. The scanner will then show a code, identifying the dog.

11

age. They're not trying to see how much money they can pry out of you; it's more likely that they're unsure of the final relative quality level of the puppy within the litter.

The breeder should be able to give you a price range, however, and this may help you in your deliberations. Regarding prices, you might keep in mind than any number of dog publication articles have entertained us by figuring the "profit" on litters, based on time spent on labor, veterinarian and medical attention, stud services, advertising, and so forth.

Contrary to popular misconception of those outside the field and newcomers to dog breeding, even if everything goes right in producing a litter, the hourly payback amounts to somewhere around $1.47 per hour for the litter owner's time. It is truly a labor of love for the long-term breeder, and that's one of the reasons why the career span of the dog

Using positive reinforcement to teach your Dalmatian the proper way to walk on leash will train her to walk calmly by your side and not pull.

fancier usually lasts up to about five years maximum or is a lifetime commitment. Those people who stay "in dogs" for more than five years generally do so for the rest of their lives. Those who don't probably realize that the "dog game" has animal husbandry as its foundation (rather than profit, power, riches and fame) and get out of it before five years elapse. It's expensive when a litter winds up costing a breeder $2,000 in veterinary bills on top of a previously paid stud service, and most people who enter into dog breeding have no idea that their "tuition" might run so high, nor understand the level of responsibility required and the emotional and financial stress.

GETTING USED TO A LEASH

Your puppy will need a close-fitting nylon or cotton-webbed collar. This collar should be adjustable so that it can be used for the first couple of months. A properly fit collar is tight enough that it will not slip over the head, yet an adult finger fits easily under it. A puppy should never wear a choke chain or any other adult training collar.

In addition to a collar, you'll need a 4-to-6-foot-long leash. One made of nylon or cotton-webbed material is a fine and inexpensive first leash. It does not need to be more than $1/2$ an inch in width. It is important to make sure that the clip is of excellent quality and cannot become unclasped on its own. You will need one or two leads for walking the dog, as well as a collar or harness. If you live in a cold climate, a sweater or jacket for excursions with your Dal would be appropriate. Get a somewhat larger size than you immediately need to allow for growth.

The objective when using the lead for the first ten to twenty tries is to get the puppy used to wearing it and responding to you (to your voice direction, affection or reward) rather than to a tugging message from the collar and leash. This is your opportunity to have the puppy associate wonderful experiences with the leash. If done right, the dog will grow into one who jumps for joy every time you show the lead to her because she knows it means a walk or playtime or rewards and praise. You should practice these exercises with your Dalmatian in a fenced yard or indoors until she is comfortable on leash.

WHAT YOU'LL NEED AT HOME

When you get home, you should have, at a minimum, a fenced yard, food, bowls for food and water, lots of chew toys and a sleeping quarters enclosure.

A puppy that is sniffing and searching around in small circles may be an indication that she is ready to empty out.

A dog crate is an excellent investment and is an invaluable aid in raising a puppy. It provides a safe, quiet place where a dog can sleep. If it's used properly, a crate helps with housetraining. However, long periods of uninterrupted stays are not recommended—especially for young puppies. Unless you have someone at home or can have someone come in a few times a day to let her out to relieve herself and socialize with her for a while, a *small* crate is not advisable. Never lock a young puppy in a small crate for an entire day!

Make sure your Dalmatian will have company and companionship during the day. If the members of your family are not at home during the day, try to come home at lunchtime, let your puppy out and spend some time with her. If this isn't possible, try to get a neighbor or friend who lives close by to come spend time with the puppy. Your Dal thrives on human attention and guidance, and a puppy left alone most of the day will find ways to get your attention, most of them not so cute and many downright destructive.

HOUSEHOLD DANGERS

Curious puppies and inquisitive dogs get into trouble not because they are bad, but simply because they want to investigate the world around them. It's our job to protect our dogs from harmful substances, like the following:

In the Garage

antifreeze

garden supplies, like snail and slug bait, pesticides, fertilizers, mouse and rat poisons

In the House

cleaners, especially pine oil

perfumes, colognes, aftershaves

medications, vitamins

office and craft supplies

electric cords

chicken or turkey bones

chocolate, onions

some house and garden plants, like ivy, oleander and poinsettia

HOUSETRAINING HINTS

If you use an airline carrier or a crate as a sleeping enclosure, you'll find that this container is one that the puppy soon will voluntarily choose to crawl into for a nap. Use these as housetraining tools in the following way: For the first two to

Preparing your home for your new pet means locking up household cleaners and toxins so your Dal doesn't discover them.

four weeks of adjusting to home life, be with the puppy whenever she is loose in the house. If it looks like she has to void, take her outside or to her designated doggie toilet, and stay with her until she urinates and/ or defecates, and offer praise for success. Then bring her back into the house, still keeping her within sight. If she does not go, confine the pup to her crate and take her outside or to her toilet every hour. Only let an empty pup have supervised freedom in your home. Whenever you have to leave the room momentarily, the puppy is enclosed in the crate until you return.

If you follow this routine religiously for two to four weeks, gradually providing supervised exposure to the rest of the house, it is possible to raise a dog that never has an "accident" inside the house.

CHEW TOYS FOR YOUR PUP

Chewing is normal for puppies—it's their instinctive way of communicating within the litter and is as natural as babbling is for human babies. Excessive chewing can be partially resolved by providing a puppy with her own chew toys. Small-size dog biscuits are good for the teeth and also act as an amusing toy. Do not buy chew toys composed of compressed particles, as these particles disintegrate when chewed and can get stuck in the puppy's throat. Hard rubber or plastic toys are also good for chewing, as are large rawhide bones. Avoid the smaller chewsticks, as they can splinter and choke the puppy. Anything given to a dog must be large enough that it cannot be swallowed.

Most likely, your puppy will chew anything she can sink her teeth into. Be aware of some of the items your puppy has access to in your home and yard—they may be dangerous or deadly to your pup. Identify the vegetation you have and call your veterinarian, your county extension service or a plant expert and find out whether your plants are toxic to dogs. They will chew on rocks, too, especially ones about as big as your thumb that are fun to toss around in their mouths. If you see them doing this, take the rock from them and dispose of it. Some Dals will get carried away with sloshing them around in their mouths and before they know it, they swallow them. Keep antifreeze, slug bait, rodent poison and other toxins locked up because your curious Dal will find them, ingest them and die. There are also foods that are toxic to dogs, which are discussed in chapter 3. Teaching a Dal what is and is not permissible to chew is generally a process that lasts the lifetime of the dog. They're constantly discovering new things to chew that you've never had to pass judgment on.

If you follow the simple guidelines discussed above, your trip home should be the beginning of a wonderful adventure and a devoted partnership that will last longer than a decade.

Training your Dal to love chew toys is the most reliable way to keep her from chewing on your things.

16

CHAPTER THREE

To Good Health

FIRST THINGS FIRST

Dalmatians do not thrive on diets
high in purines (compounds found
in certain meat and vegetable proteins) and some will develop serious,
life-threatening health problems or
die prematurely as a result of such
diets. Dalmatians don't break down
purines beyond the level of uric acid,
whereas other breeds go a step further,
converting uric acid to allantoin
before excretion. This trait creates
the potential for Dalmatians to form
uratic kidney or bladder stones or
other diet-related health problems.
Luckily, several commercially manufactured dry dog foods work well for
Dalmatians.

Dalmatians seem to do well when
fed dry foods with no supplements:
a dry kibble, which is 19 percent protein, corn-based and contains a meat
component provided by chicken. Offer it twice daily, preparing it by soak-
ing it in warm water for fifteen minutes before feeding. It is important
to note that in addition to feeding
an appropriate food, make sure your
dogs always have fresh water available and get lots of exercise daily.

EXPERT ADVICE

1. Never feed a Dalmatian organ meats (such as liver, kidney, sweetbreads or brains), game meats (such as venison or elk) or red meat in any form, whether cooked, raw or as an ingredient in a pet food or snack.

2. Never feed poultry, cooked or raw, where it appears as one of the first two ingredients listed on the label.

3. Feed most fruits, vegetables and grains as snacks, except those known to be high in purine yields such as mushrooms, asparagus, legumes, oatmeal, spinach and cauliflower.

4. Feed adult Dalmatians pet foods (corn, wheat and rice, in that order) whose protein and fat content are moderate: about 22 percent protein from low purine sources and no more than 10 percent fat.

5. Divide the dog's total daily ration into two or more meals so that blood levels of uric acid will remain fairly stable. Soak meals in warm water to improve water consumption and make sure fresh water is available at all times.

Foods Yielding High Purine Levels

Highest:

- Organ meats
- Game meats
- Gravies and meat extracts
- Canned snack fishes, such as sardines and herring
- Sweetbreads

High:
- Meats: beef, veal, pork and lamb
- Poultry (poultry is not as high as red meat)
- Fish (fresh and saltwater) and shellfish
- Oatmeal, whole grains, wheat germ and legumes

Dalmatians have a breed-specific intolerance for high-purine foods.

18

- Asparagus, cauliflower, mushrooms and spinach

Lowest:
- Fruits, nuts and berries
- Dairy products
- Eggs
- Vegetables

DEAFNESS

Another limiting characteristic encountered in Dalmatians is deafness.

According to data now collected through a formal program conducted by the Dalmatian Club of America, the incidence of total deafness in Dalmatians (no hearing in either ear) is around 8 percent, and the number that hear in only one ear is about 22 percent. Breeders have become aware of this genetic defect, however, and are minimizing the problem by selective breeding.

Normal human observation couldn't detect the difference between a Dal with full hearing and one that heard in only one ear: They both act almost exactly the same. But now, unilateral deafness in Dalmatians is detectable, and it is therefore possible to eliminate them from breeding programs, by which

Aside from nutritionally sound food, your Dal's health also depends on the amount and quality of time spent with his family.

the problem could be perpetuated. Today, these partially deaf Dals are placed as pets, with breeding restrictions to limit the number of future deaf Dalmatians. These dogs make great pets, because to the pet owner and casual observer, as noted above, their behavior is indistinguishable from a dog with full hearing capacity.

SKIN PROBLEMS

Some Dals will develop allergies that are unrelated to their unique metabolism and which are found among all breeds and mixed breeds. These can arise from inhaled allergens, such as pollens and dust; from things in the

19

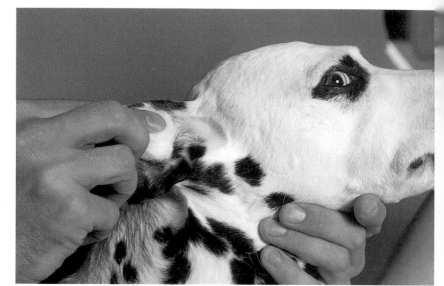

Checking your dog's ears regularly for debris and dry skin can protect your dog from ear infections and split ears.

environment, such as wool blankets; or from specific ingredients in food products or chew toys, such as wheat or leather. A good veterinary dermatologist is the person to see regarding all skin problems that are of concern to you. Let common sense guide you.

Treating Split Ears and Tails

If you are unfortunate enough to have to contend with a split ear, the best cure is inactivity. It's the same as if you had chapped lips: Don't smile. You can coat the end of the

ear with a softening agent, like vitamin E oil, but the process of healing an ear that slaps against the dog's skull every time it shakes can be a slow one. Some ear splits may be hastened in healing with liquid bandages or hoods. The bottom line, though, is that it will heal faster if the reason for the head shaking disappears.

This same skin-splitting trouble can arise with the tail of the Dal, too. The same solution applies. You can soften the skin or cover the wound with a liquid bandage (not with a cloth bandage—that will last only about five seconds once you're out of sight), and you must quiet the dog down so he doesn't have the opportunity to bang his tail against anything for a while. If the dog has sleeping quarters or nesting quarters where it is normally quiet, leave him there except for long walks on a leash—away from objects that he might hit with his tail—for a few days.

THE IMPORTANCE OF PREVENTIVE CARE

You can help your dog maintain good health by practicing the art of preventive care. Take good care of your Dalmatian today and he will be healthy tomorrow.

There are many aspects of preventive care with which Dalmatian owners should be familiar: Vaccinations, regular vet visits and eye care are just some. The advantage of preventive care is that it prevents problems.

The earlier that illness is detected in the Dalmatian, the easier it is for the veterinarian to treat the problem. Owners can help ensure their dogs' health by being on the lookout for medical problems. All this requires is an eye for detail and a willingness to observe. Pay close attention to your Dalmatian, how he looks, how he acts. What is normal behavior? How does his coat usually look? What are his eating and sleeping patterns? Subtle changes can indicate a problem. Keep close tabs on what is normal for your Dalmatian, and if anything out of the ordinary develops call the veterinarian.

Eye Problems

When eye problems occur, they usually require a trip to the vet. Dogs generally are too fidgety to allow a careful look at the eye, especially if

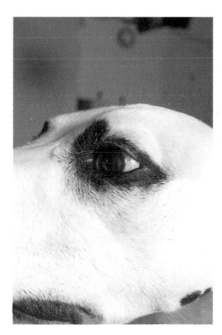

Make sure your Dal's eyes are free of irritation.

there is an irritation present. If your vet prescribes eye drops or ointment, the administration is different for each kind of medication. Eye drops may be dropped directly into the eye after securing the dog's head, pulling the lower lid down and drawing back on the skin above the eye. Ointment

ADVANTAGES OF SPAY/NEUTER

The greatest advantage of spaying (for females) or neutering (for males) your dog is that you are guaranteed your dog will not produce puppies. There are too many puppies already available for too few homes. There are other advantages as well.

Advantages of Spaying

No messy heats.

No "suitors" howling at your windows or waiting in your yard.

No risk of pyometra (disease of the uterus) and decreased incidences of mammary cancer.

Advantages of Neutering

Decreased incidences of fighting, but does not affect the dog's personality.

Decreased roaming in search of bitches in season.

Decreased incidences of many urogenital diseases.

should be squeezed out and placed in the lower lid, not dropped in the eye. The lower lid can then be massaged to spread the ointment around.

Spaying and Neutering

Spaying or neutering—surgically altering the Dalmatian so it cannot reproduce—should be at the top of every owner's "To Do" list. Why?

First, every day thousands of puppies are born in the United States as a result of uncontrolled breeding. For every pet living in a happy home today, there are four pets on the street or in abusive homes suffering from starvation, exposure, neglect or mistreatment. In six years, a single female dog and her offspring can be the source of 67,000 new dogs.

A second reason to spay or neuter your Dalmatian is to create a healthier, more well-adjusted pet that, in most cases, will live longer than an intact animal. A spayed female is no longer susceptible to pyometra (infection of the uterus), and is less prone to mammary cancers. The procedure eliminates the behavior that accompanies the female's heat cycle. A neutered male is less likely to develop prostate or anal cancer and is less apt to roam.

Marking behavior is also reduced by altering.

When should your Dalmatian be spayed or neutered? Recommendations vary among vets, but 6 months of age is commonly suggested. Ask your vet what age is best for your Dalmatian.

Vaccinations

Another priority on a Dalmatian owner's list of preventive care is vaccinations. Vaccinations protect the dog against a host of infectious diseases, preventing an illness itself and the misery that accompanies it.

Vaccines should be a part of every young puppy's health care, since youngsters are so susceptible to disease. To remain effective, vaccinations must be kept current.

Good Nutrition

Dogs that receive the appropriate nutrients daily will be healthier and stronger than those that do not. The proper balance of proteins, fats, carbohydrates, vitamins, minerals and sufficient water enables the dog to remain healthy by fighting off illness.

Routine Checkups

Regular visits to the veterinary clinic should begin when your Dalmatian is a young pup and continue throughout his life. Make this a habit and it will certainly contribute to your Dal's good health. Even if your Dalmatian seems perfectly healthy, a checkup once or twice a year is in order. Even if your dog seems fine to you, he could have an ongoing problem. Your veterinarian is trained to notice subtle changes or hints of illness.

23

Because your Dalmatian will inevitably take some risks during his lifetime, you'll want to keep your dog on leash when going outside.

Well-Being

Aside from the dog's physical needs—a proper and safe shelter, nutritious diet, health care and regular exercise—the Dalmatian needs plenty of plain, old-fashioned love. The dog is happiest when he is part of a family, enjoying the social interactions, nurturing and play. Bringing the Dalmatian into the family provides him with a sense of security.

COMMON DISEASES

Unfortunately, even with the best preventive care, the Dalmatian can fall ill. Infectious diseases, which are commonly spread from dog to dog via infected urine, feces or other body secretions, can wreak havoc. Following are a few of the diseases that can affect your Dalmatian.

Rabies

Probably one of the most well-known diseases that can affect dogs, rabies can strike any warm-blooded animal (including humans)—and is fatal. The rabies virus, which is present in an affected animal's saliva, is usually spread through a bite or open wound. The signs of the disease can be subtle at first. Normally friendly pets can become irritable and withdrawn. Shy pets may become overly friendly. Eventually, the dog becomes withdrawn and avoids light, which hurts the eyes of a rabid dog. Fever, vomiting and diarrhea are common.

Once these symptoms develop, the animal will die; there is no treatment or cure.

Since rabid animals may have a tendency to be aggressive and bite, animals suspected of having rabies should only be handled by animal control handlers or veterinarians.

Rabies is preventable with routine vaccines, and such vaccinations are required by law for domestic animals in all states in this country.

Parvovirus

Canine parvovirus is a highly contagious and devastating illness. The hardy virus is usually transmitted through contaminated feces, but it can be carried on an infected dog's feet or skin. It strikes dogs of all ages and is most serious in young puppies.

There are two main types of parvovirus. The first signs of the diarrhea-syndrome type are usually depression and lack of appetite, followed by vomiting and the characteristic bloody diarrhea. The dog appears to be in great pain, and he usually has a high fever.

The cardiac-syndrome type affects the heart muscle and is most common in young puppies. Puppies with this condition will stop nursing, whine and gasp for air. Death may occur suddenly or in a few days. Youngsters that recover can have lingering heart failure that eventually takes their life.

Veterinarians can treat dogs with parvovirus, but the outcome varies. It depends on the age of the animal and severity of the disease. Treatment may include fluid therapy, medication to stop the severe diarrhea and antibiotics to prevent or stop secondary infection.

Young puppies receive some antibody protection against the disease from their mother, but they lose it quickly and must be vaccinated to prevent the disease. In most cases, vaccinated puppies are protected against the disease.

Coronavirus

Canine coronavirus is especially devastating to young puppies, causing depression, lack of appetite,

YOUR PUPPY'S VACCINES

Vaccines are given to prevent your dog from getting infectious diseases like canine distemper or rabies. Vaccines are the ultimate preventive medicine: They're given before your dog ever gets the disease so as to protect him from the disease. That's why it is necessary for your dog to be vaccinated routinely. Puppy vaccines start at 8 weeks of age for the five-in-one DHLPP vaccine and are given every three to four weeks until the puppy is 16 months old. Your veterinarian will put your puppy on a proper schedule and will remind you when to bring in your dog for shots.

vomiting that may contain blood and characteristically yellow-orange diarrhea. The virus is transmitted through feces, urine and saliva, and the onset of symptoms is usually rapid.

Dogs suffering from coronavirus are treated similarly to those suffering from parvovirus: fluid therapy, medication to stop diarrhea and vomiting and antibiotics if necessary.

Vaccinations are available to protect puppies and dogs against the virus and are recommended especially for those dogs in frequent contact with other dogs.

Distemper

Caused by a virus, distemper is highly contagious and is most common in unvaccinated puppies aged 3 to 8 months, but older dogs are susceptible as well. Luckily, because of modern-day vaccinations, this disease is no longer the killer it was 50 years ago.

It is especially important to vaccinate bitches for distemper before breeding to ensure maternal antibodies in the pups.

Hepatitis

Infectious canine hepatitis can affect dogs of every age, but it is most severe in puppies. It primarily affects the dog's liver, kidneys and lining of the blood vessels. Highly contagious, it is transmitted through urine, feces and saliva.

This disease has several forms. In the fatal fulminating form, the dog becomes ill very suddenly, develops bloody diarrhea and dies. In the acute form, the dog develops a fever, has bloody diarrhea, vomits blood and refuses to eat. Jaundice may be present; the whites of the dog's eyes appear yellow. Dogs with a mild case are lethargic or depressed and often refuse to eat.

Infectious canine hepatitis must be diagnosed and confirmed with a blood test. Ill dogs require hospitalization. Hepatitis is preventable in dogs by keeping vaccinations current.

Lyme Disease

Lyme disease has received a lot of press recently, with its increased incidence throughout the United States. The illness, caused by the bacteria *Borrelia burgdorferi*, is carried by ticks. It is passed along when the tick bites a victim, canine or human. (The dog cannot pass the disease to people, though. It is only transmitted via the tick.) It is most common during the tick season in May through August.

In dogs, the disease manifests itself in sudden lameness, caused by swollen joints, similar to arthritis. The dog is weak and may run a fever. The lameness can last a few days or several months, and some dogs have recurring difficulties.

Three types of ticks (l-r): the wood tick, brown dog tick and deer tick.

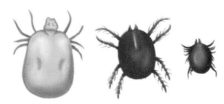

Antibiotics are very effective in treating Lyme disease, and the sooner it is diagnosed and treated, the better. A vaccine is available; ask your veterinarian if your dog would benefit from it.

Kennel Cough

"Kennel cough," or "canine cough," shows itself as a harsh, dry cough. This contagious disease has been termed "kennel cough," much to the dismay of kennel owners, because of its often rapid spread through kennels. The cough may persist for weeks and is often followed by a bout of chronic bronchitis.

Many kennels require proof of bordatella vaccination before boarding. If your dog is in and out of kennels frequently, vaccination certainly is not a bad idea.

FIRST AID

First aid is not a substitute for professional care, though it can help save a dog's life.

To Stop Bleeding

Bleeding from a severe cut or wound must be stopped right away. There

WHEN TO CALL THE VETERINARIAN

In any emergency situation, you should call your veterinarian immediately. Try to stay calm when you call, and give the vet or the assistant as much information as possible before you leave for the clinic. That way, the staff will be able to take immediate, specific action when you arrive. Emergencies include:

- Bleeding or deep wounds
- Hyperthermia (overheating)
- Shock
- Dehydration
- Abdominal pain
- Burns
- Fits
- Unconsciousness
- Broken bones
- Paralysis

Call your veterinarian if you suspect any health troubles.

are two basic techniques—direct pressure and the tourniquet.

Try to control bleeding first by using direct pressure. Ask an assistant to hold the injured Dalmatian

POISON ALERT

If your dog has ingested a potentially poisonous substance, waste no time. Call the National Animal Poison Control Center hot line:

(800) 548-2423 ($30 per case) or

(900) 680-0000 ($20 first five minutes; $2.95 each additional minute)

and place several pads of sterile gauze over the wound. Press. Do not wipe the wound or apply any cleansers or ointments. Apply firm, even pressure. If blood soaks through the pad, do not remove it as this could disrupt clotting. Simply place another pad on top and continue to apply pressure.

If bleeding on a leg or the tail does not stop by applying pressure, try using a tourniquet. Use this only as a last resort. A tourniquet that is left on too long can result in limb loss.

If the dog is bleeding from his mouth or anus, or vomits or defecates blood, he may be suffering from internal injuries. Do not attempt to stop bleeding. Call the veterinarian right away for emergency treatment.

Poisoning

A dog's curiosity will often lead him to eat or lick things he shouldn't. Unfortunately, many substances are poisonous to dogs, including household products, plants or chemicals. Owners must learn to act quickly if poisoning is suspected because the results can be deadly.

If your dog appears to be poisoned:

- Call your veterinarian and follow his or her directions.

- Try to identify the poison source— this is really important. Take the container or plant to the clinic.

Heatstroke

Heatstroke can be deadly and must be treated immediately to save the dog. Signs include rapid panting, darker-than-usual gums and tongue, salivating, exhaustion or vomiting. The dog's body temperature is elevated, sometimes as high as 106°F. If the dog is not treated, coma and death can follow.

If heatstroke is suspected, cool down your overheated dog as quickly as possible. Mildly affected dogs can be moved to a cooler environment,

28

into an air-conditioned home, for example, or wrapped in moistened towels. Call your veterinarian.

Insect Bites/Stings

Just like people, dogs can suffer bee stings and insect bites. Bees, wasps and yellow jackets leave a nasty, painful sting, and if your dog is stung repeatedly shock can occur.

If an insect bite is suspected, try to identify the culprit. Remove the stinger if it is a bee sting, and apply a mixture of baking soda and water to the sting. It is also a good idea to apply ice packs to reduce inflammation and ease pain. Call your veterinarian, especially if your dog seems ill or goes into shock.

INTERNAL PARASITES

Dogs are susceptible to several internal parasites. Keeping your Dalmatian free of internal parasites is another important aspect of health care.

Watch for general signs of poor condition: a dull coat, weight loss, lethargy, coughing, weakness and diarrhea.

For proper diagnosis and treatment of internal parasites, consult a veterinarian.

Roundworms

Roundworms, or ascarids, are probably the most common worms that affect dogs. Most puppies are born with these organisms in their intestines, which is why youngsters are treated for these parasites as soon as it is safe to do so.

Animals contract roundworms by ingesting infected soil and feces. A roundworm infestation can rob vital nutrients from young puppies and even cause diarrhea, vomiting and digestive upset. Roundworms can also harm a young animal's liver and lungs, so treatment is imperative.

Tapeworms

Tapeworms are commonly transmitted by fleas to dogs. Tapeworm eggs enter the body of a canine host when the animal accidentally ingests a carrier flea. The parasite settles in the intestines, where it sinks its head into the intestinal wall and feeds off material the host is digesting. The worm grows a body of egg packets, which break off periodically and are expelled from the body in the feces. Fleas then ingest the eggs from the feces and the parasite's life cycle begins all over again.

29

THE ESSENTIAL DALMATIAN

WHAT'S WRONG WITH MY DOG?

We've listed some common conditions of health problems and their possible causes. If any of the following conditions appear serious or persist for more than 24 hours, make an appointment to see your veterinarian immediately.

CONDITIONS	POSSIBLE CAUSES
DIARRHEA	Intestinal upset, typically caused by eating something bad or overeating. Can also be a viral infection, a bad case of nerves or anxiety or a parasite infection. If you see blood in the feces, get to the vet right away.
VOMITING/RETCHING	Dogs regurgitate fairly regularly (bitches for their young), whenever something upsets their stomachs, or even out of excitement or anxiety. Often dogs eat grass, which, because it's indigestible in its pure form, irritates their stomachs and causes them to vomit. Getting a good look at *what* your dog vomited can better indicate what's causing it.
COUGHING	Obstruction in the throat; virus (kennel cough); roundworm infestation; congestive heart failure.
RUNNY NOSE	Because dogs don't catch colds like people, a runny nose is a sign of congestion or irritation.
LOSS OF APPETITE	Because most dogs are hearty and regular eaters, a loss of appetite can be your first and most accurate sign of a serious problem.
LOSS OF ENERGY (LETHARGY)	Any number of things could be slowing down your dog, from an infection to internal tumors to overexercise—even overeating.

30

Hookworms

Hookworms are so named because they hook onto an animal's small intestine and suck the host's blood. Like roundworms, hookworms are contracted when a dog ingests contaminated soil or feces.

Hookworms can be especially devastating to dogs. They will become thin and sick; puppies can die. An affected dog will suffer from

CONDITIONS	POSSIBLE CAUSES
STINKY BREATH	Imagine if you never brushed your teeth! Foul-smelling breath indicates plaque and tartar buildup that could possibly have caused infection. Start brushing your dog's teeth.
LIMPING	This could be caused by something as simple as a hurt or bruised pad, to something as complicated as hip dysplasia, torn ligaments or broken bones.
CONSTANT ITCHING	Probably due to fleas, mites or an allergic reaction to food or environment (your vet will need to help you determine what your dog's allergic to).
RED, INFLAMED, ITCHY SPOTS	Often referred to as "hot spots," these are particularly common on coated breeds. They're caused by a bacterial infection that gets aggravated as the dog licks and bites at the spot.
BALD SPOTS	These are the result of excessive itching or biting at the skin so that the hair follicles are damaged; excessively dry skin; mange; calluses; and even infections. You need to determine what the underlying cause is.
STINKY EARS/HEAD SHAKING	Take a look under your dog's ear flap. Do you see brown, waxy buildup? Clean the ears with something soft and a special cleaner, and don't use cotton swabs or go too deep into the ear canal.
UNUSUAL LUMPS	Could be fatty tissue, could be something serious (infection, trauma, tumor). Don't wait to find out.

bloody diarrhea and, if the parasites migrate to the lungs, the dog may contract bronchitis or pneumonia, too.

Hookworms commonly strike puppies 2 to 8 weeks of age and are less common in adult dogs.

Whipworms

Known for their thread-like appearance, whipworms attach into the wall of the large intestine to feed. Thick-shelled eggs are passed in the feces and in about two to four weeks are mature and able to reinfect a host that ingests the eggs.

Mild whipworm infestation is often without signs, but as the worms grow, weight loss, bloody diarrhea and anemia follow. In areas where the soil is heavily contaminated, frequent checks are advised to prevent severe infestation.

Heartworms

Heartworm larvae are transmitted by the ordinary mosquito, but the effects are far from ordinary. In three to four months, the larvae

(microfilaria) become small worms and make their way to a vein, where they are transported to the heart, where they grow and reproduce.

At first, a dog with heartworms is free of symptoms. The signs vary, but the most common is a deep cough and shortness of breath. The dog tires easily, is weak and loses weight. Eventually, the dog may suffer from congestive heart failure.

EXTERNAL PARASITES

FLEAS—Besides carrying tapeworm larvae, fleas bite and suck the host's blood. Their bites itch and are extremely annoying to dogs, especially if the dog is hypersensitive to the bite. Fleas must be eliminated on the dog with special shampoos and dips. Fleas also infest the dog's bedding and the owner's home and yard.

TICKS—Several varieties of ticks attach themselves to dogs, where they burrow into the skin and suck blood. Ticks can be carriers of several diseases, including Lyme disease and Rocky Mountain Spotted Fever.

FLEAS AND TICKS

There are so many safe, effective products available now to combat fleas and ticks that—thankfully—they are less of a problem. Prevention is key, however. Ask your veterinarian about starting your puppy on a flea/tick repellent right away. With this, regular grooming and environmental controls, your dog and your home should stay pest-free. Without this attention, you risk infesting your dog and your home, and you're in for an ugly and costly battle to clear up the problem.

LICE—Lice are not common in dogs, but when they are present they cause intense irritation and itching. There are two types: biting and sucking. Biting lice feed on skin scales, and sucking lice feed on blood.

MITES—There are several types of mites that cause several kinds of mange, including sarcoptic, demodectic and cheyletiella. These microscopic mites cause intense itching and misery to the dog.

PREVENTIVE CARE PAYS

Using common sense, paying attention to your dog and working with your veterinarian, you can minimize health risks and problems. Use vet-recommended flea, tick and heartworm preventive medications; feed a nutritious diet appropriate for your dog's size, age and activity level; give your dog sufficient exercise and regular grooming; train and socialize your dog; keep current on your dog's shots; and enjoy all the years you have with your friend.

33

CHAPTER FOUR

Positively Nutritious

It's so easy to let your Dalmatian get fat.

She seems like an active dog—the marathon runner/gymnast of the dog world—that wouldn't tend toward obesity, but with the variety of low-cost foods on the market that use animal fat for taste and filler elements to provide bulk, it's no wonder that our dogs can grow up looking like fast-food junkies.

EATING RIGHT FROM THE START

Puppies need at least three meals a day through the teething stage, which occurs at about 4 months of age. Continue the three meals per day routine up to 5 or 6 months, at which time you make the switch

Stainless steel food and water bowls are the most sterile.

to two meals a day. Adults should remain on two meals per day.

SWITCHING FOODS

The puppies eat growth formula food for nine months to a year, which dog food manufacturers package as a puppy meal. When Dalmatians have grown to the developmental level at which the protein percentage in the puppy food is too high for them (which will happen to every Dal), switch to a kibble with 19 percent protein derived from low-purine food sources. Because Dalmatians are prone to developing kidney stones, it is important to follow these nutritional guidelines. (The health chapter contains a more detailed discussion on food and nutritional risks for Dalmatians.)

GROWTH STAGE FOODS

Once upon a time, there was puppy food and there was adult dog food. Now there are foods for puppies, young adults/active dogs, less active dogs and senior citizens. What's the difference between these foods? They vary by the amounts of nutrients they provide for the dog's growth stage/activity level.

Less active dogs don't need as much protein or fat as growing, active dogs; senior dogs don't need some of the nutrients vital to puppies. By feeding a high-quality food that's appropriate for your dog's age and activity level, you're benefiting your dog and yourself. Feed too much protein to a couch potato and she'll have energy to spare, which means a few more trips around the block will be needed to burn it off. Feed an adult diet to a puppy, and risk growth and development abnormalities that could affect her for a lifetime.

If you are unsure of what your Dal's nutritional needs are, buy a dog food geared for the stage of life she is in: puppy, adolescent, adult, senior.

TO SUPPLEMENT OR NOT TO SUPPLEMENT?

If you're feeding your dog a diet that's correct for her developmental stage and she's alert, healthy looking and neither over- nor underweight, you don't need to add supplements. These include table scraps as well as vitamins and minerals. In fact, unless you are a nutrition expert, using food supplements can actually hurt a growing puppy. For example, mixing too much calcium into your dog's food can lead to musculoskeletal disorders. Educating yourself about the quantity of vitamins and minerals your dog needs to be healthy will help you determine what needs to be supplemented. If you have any concerns about the nutritional quality of the food you're feeding, discuss them with your veterinarian.

HOW MUCH?

How much to feed varies from dog to dog, and also varies depending on the dog's age. Youngsters will burn up more energy than old-timers, and smaller dogs will generally eat less than larger ones. You want your dog to look trim, (but not skinny) and athletic-looking, with the last rib barely visible about the time the next feeding rolls around. Adults eat anywhere from six to nine cups of kibble per day (the total of both feedings), depending on age, sex, time of year and individual level of activity. Once they get to middle age (around 6 to 8 years), they tend to put on weight more easily than the youngsters, too. You will have to find the amount of food that produces the weight that looks best on your dog.

DEPENDING ON YOU TO FEED THEM RIGHT

What they really need, since they're domesticated creatures dependent on you for their health and longevity, is an owner who loves them enough to understand what the dog's body and activities are telling them. Keep an eye on firmness of muscle tone, look for minimal shedding, a blemish-free coat, brightness of eyes, a cool, wet nose and the normal energy level for your dog. You can get all of these qualities on a very basic feeding program with commercially prepared food, provided you know what you are looking for and properly match the food with the age and activity level of the dog.

TYPES OF FOODS/ TREATS

There are three types of commercially available dog food—dry, canned and semimoist—and a huge assortment of treats (lucky dogs!) to feed your dog. Which should you choose?

Dry and canned foods contain similar ingredients. The primary difference between them is their moisture content. The moisture is not just water. It's blood and broth,

HOW MANY MEALS A DAY?

Individual dogs vary in how much they should eat to maintain a desired body weight—not too fat, but not too thin. Puppies need several meals a day, while older dogs may need only one. Determine how much food keeps your adult dog looking and feeling her best. Then decide how many meals you want to feed with that amount. Like us, most dogs love to eat, and offering two meals a day is more enjoyable for them. If you're worried about overfeeding, make sure you measure correctly and abstain from adding tidbits to the meals.

Whether you feed one or two meals, only leave your dog's food out for the amount of time it takes her to eat it—ten minutes, for example. Free-feeding (when food is available any time) and leisurely meals encourage picky eating. Don't worry if your dog doesn't finish all her dinner in the allotted time. She'll learn she should.

37

too, the very things that dogs adore. So while canned food is more palatable, dry food is more economical, convenient and effective in controlling tartar buildup. Most owners feed a 25 percent canned/75 percent dry diet to give their dogs the benefit of both. Just be sure your dog is getting the nutrition she needs (you and your veterinarian can determine this).

How much you feed your dog depends on her stage of life and activity level.

Semimoist foods have the flavor dogs love and the convenience owners want. However, they tend to contain excessive amounts of artificial colors and preservatives.

Dog treats come in every size, shape and flavor imaginable, from organic cookies shaped like postmen to beefy chew sticks. Dogs seem to love them all, so enjoy the variety. Just be sure not to overindulge your dog. Factor treats into her regular meal sizes.

FOOD ALLERGIES

If your puppy or dog seems to itch all the time for no apparent reason, she could be allergic to one or more ingredients in her food. This is not uncommon, and it's why many foods contain lamb and rice instead of beef, wheat or soy. Have your dog tested by your veterinarian, and be patient while you strive to identify and eliminate the allergens from your dog's food (or environment).

CHAPTER FIVE

Putting on the Dog

Grooming your Dalmatian? What's to groom? Because there's little coat to dress or otherwise style for a show, grooming is less trouble with a Dal than with many other breeds. But that doesn't mean there's nothing to it, and it also doesn't mean that Dals who don't go to shows don't need grooming. They all need some basic care and they all love the extra attention that habitual grooming provides.

COAT

First of all you will notice, especially if you live in an area where it rains a lot, that all Dalmatians are mud magicians. They can get rain-soaked and covered with mud, or collect grass stains and brambles, but if you give them a half hour in a clean, dry and padded sleeping area, they come out looking brand-new. The only things that we've observed as permanent coat stains are real paint and black walnut husk stains. Otherwise, they keep themselves clean nearly year-round.

40

These well-groomed Dals make a pretty picture.

When you're getting ready for a show or a visit from Grandma, you'll probably want to put some finishing touches on your already stunning-looking pet. To do this, first shampoo with a pH-balanced shampoo in cool or tepid water. Some Dals take to water, some don't. You can bathe them in your shower, bathtub, an outside tub, or under an outside hose if it's warm enough. It's better in all cases if you have a nozzle that sprays a gentle shower and doesn't make a lot of noise. Wash the dog as you would your own hair: Wet down, lather, rinse and repeat. Rinse thoroughly so you get all the soap out—then stand back for the dog to shake from nose to tail, after which you can dry him off with a thick cloth towel.

After the shower, do you notice discoloration or reddish stains in the wrinkles or lip of the dog's lower jaw? Do you notice any redness in the spots or lumps anywhere on the dog? How about the skin on the underside? Is it smooth, blemish-free and light pink, or almost white? The red blemishes or shading in wrinkled areas are not a sign of dirt, but more likely an indication that the dog's diet might possibly need some adjustment. Dals, like other breeds and humans, can have allergies to specific things in their environment, but reddishness in the lower lip, on top of the head or elsewhere on the body should merit a consideration of food first.

If it is feasible, after using the towel, your dog should be able to run in the house or a clean area to dry the rest of the moisture from its skin. After drying the dog completely, finish the grooming by clipping or grinding toenails, trimming whiskers and the loin area, and by thinning or trimming cowlicks and the tail as necessary.

TOENAILS

The nails on all feet should be kept short enough so they do not touch the ground when the dog walks.

Dogs with long nails can have difficulty walking on hard or slick surfaces. This can be especially true of older dogs. As nails grow longer,

QUICK AND PAINLESS NAIL CLIPPING

This is possible if you make a habit out of handling your dog's feet and giving your dog treats when you do. When it's time to clip nails, go through the same routine, but take your clippers and snip off just the ends of the nail—clip too far down and you'll cut into the "quick," the nerve center, hurting your dog and causing the nail to bleed. Clip two nails a session while you're getting your dog used to the procedure, and you'll soon be doing all four feet quickly and easily.

41

the only way the foot can compensate and retain balance is for the toes themselves to spread apart, causing the foot itself to become flattened and splayed.

Nails that are allowed to become long are also more prone to splitting. This is painful to the dog and usually requires surgical removal of the remainder of the nail for proper healing to occur.

You must clip your dog's nails regularly. Begin cutting your puppy's nails early on—hold him on your lap and play with his feet. Handle them, stroke them, get him accustomed to having them touched. Make sure you

Teaching your dog to sit for toe-nail sessions and to expect a treat and oodles of praise when finished will produce an unafraid and calm Dalmatian.

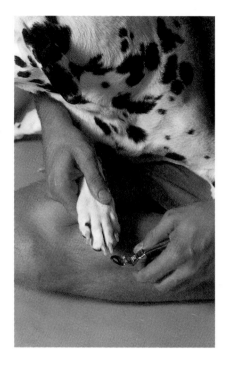

on the Dalmatian's nail. But if you misjudge and the nail bleeds, use a styptic powder to stop it. Place the powder on the nail, applying gentle pressure.

If you can't manage the nails yourself, have your veterinarian clip them. Nails that are too long throw the dog off balance and may cause back problems. Also, if the nail is too long, it will eventually turn inward, which makes it difficult to cut because of the proximity to the pad. If that is the case, let your veterinarian do it.

GETTING USED TO THE GRIND

The tools for adult dog toenail care include grinders of the Dremel hobby type, equipped with a sandpaper drum, or mechanical clippers of the Resco type. If you use a grinder, expose the puppy as early as possible to the grinder itself first, and then to the noise of the grinder while you are using it for another task. Start with a low-volume noise that approximates the grinder and work your way up to to full speed with the puppy in the room. You then work up to holding the puppy while you have the grinder in use (protect the

praise him often. Also, rub the nail clippers across his paws. Let him smell them, and feel them, all the while telling him they won't hurt him. Speak to him in soothing tones and gently take hold of his paw and barely tip the nail. Go slowly and stop before he starts to object. If he begins to pull away, correct him gently and do one more nail before you stop. At the end of each session, give him a treat.

You need only cut the tips of the nails off. It is difficult to see the quick puppy's eyes from any danger) and finally, to touching the dog with the running grinder and working your way toward exposing his feet to it.

If you are careful and persistent, and if you stay away from the quick while grinding, you should have a cooperative toenail patient forever. The three things that bother the dogs about the grinder the most are the whine of the motor, the vibration of the drum on the toenail, and being restrained for the job. With all three of these factors, the later the dog is introduced to toenail grinding, the greater the fear becomes.

COAT TRIMMING

With regard to cowlicks, the Dal typically has three areas that may require attention before entering the show ring. They are located at the front of the chest, the hip points of the buttocks, and from the bottom insertion point of the ear down the neck. All of these areas, when trimmed with a thinning scissors (teeth on one blade, cutting blade on the other), produce a smoother look which gives a subtle advantage in the show ring. The cowlicks at the breastbone run horizontally from the outside of the shoulders toward the center of the

GROOMING TOOLS

- pin brush
- slicker brush
- flea comb
- towel
- mat rake
- grooming glove
- scissors
- nail clippers
- tooth-cleaning equipment
- shampoo
- conditioner
- clippers

43

breastbone. To trim these areas, hold the scissors parallel to the cowlick ridge and thin it down to get rid of the ridge. The breastbone itself may have a cowlick, too. Thin it so the ridge disappears.

The same advice applies to the cowlicks on the rear. The object is to simply smooth down the hairline. The hair also tends to grow a little long and feathery along the backs of the legs from the hocks to about midway up the thighs. The thinning scissors can smooth this area, too. As for the tail, not all Dals have the same length of coat, so you may not need any more trimming than just to smooth the cowlick at the end of the tail.

Sometimes, however, the tail may need thinning on the underside for about the last two-thirds of its length, which thinning scissors will take care of. When you trim the tail, make sure that when viewed from the side it tapers gracefully from the base of the tail to the very tip. It must be smooth, stong-looking and without a visible break from base to tip.

Trimming the loin area cleans up the underline. There is a fold of skin that extends from the front of the thigh to the rib cage when the dog is standing in a show stack position. This skin fold is either shaped with an electric clipper or trimmed with a curved-blade, blunt-nosed scissors to make the line along the bottom of this skin fold clean.

If the dog has redness between the toes or in the wrinkles of the mouth, a peroxide wash may help, and corn-starch has been used to lighten up the skin discoloration underlying the coat. The problem, though, may be one of nutrition rather than shampoo or coat conditioning.

With regard to whiskers, remember that they are found over the eyes; on the sides of the mouth and on each cheek; under the jaws in the center; and a little farther back at each side. Trim them off for a clean look.

You may have read that if you trim your dog's whiskers, he'll either lose his balance or not be quite as smart as dogs with whiskers. You may also have heard that if you trim puppies' whiskers they won't com-pletely develop mentally. This is based on the fact that whiskers provide a

44

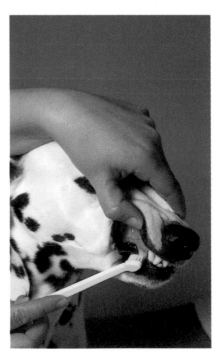

Brushing your Dal's teeth and checking his gums should also be a part of your regular grooming regimen.

Part of caring for your Dal is to make sure he has a wagging tail, a confident attitude and boundless energy to run and play until he wears you out.

sense of touch, which tells animals whether they can stick their heads or entire bodies down a varmint hole, or let them know how close they are to objects in their environment (much like the little feeler spring wires that attach to the fenders of automobiles, which alert drivers to curbs).

Trimming whiskers on Dalmatians does nothing to make them clumsier or measurably dumber than other dogs. In fact, you could probably shave their entire bodies and still wind up with Dals smarter than about 90 percent of the other breeds. Smartness has never been a Dal problem (unless you happen to disagree with their conclusions—and that's really your problem, not theirs).

Now that you have a Dal that is sparkling clean, properly trimmed and ready to make the rest of the dog world pale by comparison, the only things left to complete the picture are the wagging tail, a distinguished and confident attitude, and boundless energy to run and play until you are completely worn out.

CHAPTER SIX

Measuring Up

Dalmatians are magicians, success-fully adapting to a wide range of owners' lifestyles—from high-energy activities to relaxing with their families. Their uniqueness, as observed by each owner, stems from their at-tentiveness to, and preference for, human companionship. Despite their athleticism and ability to be on the go all day long, they'd really like nothing better than to be with their owners.

47

THE SAME, BUT DIFFERENT

Aside from the unique relationships they develop with their owners,

A black-spotted Dalmatian.

though, they're all the same, right? Well, not exactly. Granted, they are dogs with black or liver (dark brown) spots on white coats; are medium-sized, weighing about 45 to 65 pounds and measuring 19 to 24 inches in height at the withers. But if you look closer, individual Dalmatians vary in looks as much as individual humans do.

One way Dalmatians keep looking like Dalmatians is through the use of the American Kennel Club registry system and adherence by breeders to a written "breed standard," which protects and promotes the interests of each specific breed. The

A liver-spotted Dalmatian.

standard enables breeders of all dogs to compare their breeding efforts to a written description of a "perfect example" of what a dog of the breed should look like, how she should act and what she should be able to do.

STUDYING THE STANDARD

The *general appearance* emphasis on distinctive appearance, poise, alertness, lack of shyness and an intelligent expression relates directly to the Dal's human orientation and coach-dog duties. The Dal was selected with an emphasis on service and eye-catching appearance. She had to have the self-confidence to be among people, vehicles, horses and the clatter of the streets without losing composure or attention to her duty, which was to protect the horses and clear the path for safe and swift passage of the carriage.

LOOKS AND ACTION

The Dalmatian's distinctive markings have also been preserved by careful breeding programs throughout history. The spotted coat not only sets Dals apart from all other breeds, but if you think of the

Genetically, the Dal is a solid black- or liver-colored animal that also carries a gene for covering over the black or liver color. This "white masking of the black or liver base color" shows up in looks ranging from torn splotches of dark color to perfectly round dots of varying sizes.

49

rough-and-tumble aspects of her fire wagon escort work, it's obvious that her tasks were easier when "road obstacles" saw her coming and knew what she had in mind.

The Dalmatian does what she does because she loves to do it. It's in her blood. Only after she's done her work and after the carriage has stopped, will you find her nestled on top of the rig next to the driver. What about today with no carriages to speak of and cars that go too fast for Dal escorts? Well, joggers know that Dalmatians will run farther than other breeds of dogs, and will still keep that "intelligent expression" and "Can I go again?" look even though their tongues may be hanging three feet long. Fatigue, age, cars, squirrels, people and bird distractions—none of it matters. It's in the blood, and it's there from the start.

The *general appearance* also asks for a dog that is not exaggerated or coarse and is symmetrical in outline. The standard reflects that coarseness of a coat does not lend itself to the nimbleness and quickness found in a Dal or the required distance running. The symmetrical outline contributes to ease of movement in endurance situations. Combined with the size requirements, these standards produce a dog that has one of the highest

agility-to-strength ratios in the entire dog world.

BALANCE AND SYMMETRY

The Dalmatian is a balanced-looking, symmetrical dog. She was bred to run effortlessly, with endurance and a fair amount of speed. The symmetry assists in this process.

It is desirable to have a Dalmatian that is 19 to 23 inches at the withers. Dogs under or over these dimensions are faulted for being too short or too tall. A Dalmatian with proper size and proportion will run the socks off another that's over 24 inches at the withers.

To give a more accurate description of what the standard calls for in each of the Dalmatian's features, excerpts from the standard as it appears in the *AKC Complete Dog Book, 19th Edition Revised* have been emphasized in italics below.

Head

The head is in balance with the overall dog. It is of fair length and is free of loose skin. The Dalmatian's expression is alert and intelligent, indicating a stable and outgoing temperament.

The Dal's expression is alert and intelligent.

When you read the standard's head section, it looks almost like an artful dodge. What is fair length and free of loose skin? What's an alert, intelligent expression and what is this "balance" thing again? Maybe one of the best ways to think about balance and expression is to remember that Walt Disney's artists spent literally hundreds of hours with many Dalmatians before they started drawing them for the animated classic, *101 Dalmatians.*

The Dalmatian is a paragon of balance and moderation. You don't want a big head on a little dog or vice versa. Similarly, you don't want an extremely elegant head on a male dog or a very "doggy" (remember the coarseness comments) head on a bitch. Again, this has to do with size and balance, and to some extent with sex. The females are generally more feminine versions of the males and this male/female difference should be apparent. The head should have clean lines and the Dalmatian should have a clean (not drooling or loose-lipped) mouth.

WHAT IS A BREED STANDARD?

A breed standard—a detailed description of an individual breed—is meant to portray the ideal specimen of that breed. This includes ideal structure, temperament, gait, type—all aspects of the dog. Because the standard describes an ideal specimen, it isn't based on any particular dog. It is a concept against which judges compare actual dogs and breeders strive to produce dogs. At a dog show, the dog that wins is the one that comes closest, in the judge's opinion, to the standard for its breed. Breed standards are written by the breed parent clubs, the national organizations formed to oversee the well-being of the breed. They are voted on and approved by the members of the parent clubs.

51

Eyes

The eyes are set moderately well apart, are medium sized and somewhat rounded in appearance, and are set well into the skull. Eye color is brown or blue, or any combination thereof; the darker the better and usually in black-spotted rather than in liver-spotted dogs.

Ears

The ears are of moderate size, proportionately wide at the base and gradually tapering to a rounded tip. They are set rather high, and are carried close to the head, and are thin and fine in texture.

Skull

The top of the skull is flat with a slight vertical furrow and is approximately as wide as it is long. The stop is moderately well defined. The cheeks blend smoothly into a powerful muzzle, the top of which is level and parallel to the top of the skull. The muzzle and the top of the skull are about equal in length.

Nose

The nose is completely pigmented on the leather, black in black-spotted dogs and brown in liver-spotted dogs. Incomplete nose pigment is a major fault.

Lips

The lips are clean and close fitting. The teeth meet in a scissors bite. Overshot or undershot bites are disqualifications.

Neck, Topline, Body

This segment calls for a smooth (no excess skin folds) throat and a *nicely arched, fairly long neck.* The word "arched" denotes a curved structure: A Dal's **neck** is not a stovepipe. The *topline is smooth,* without a dip or break between the withers and the back.

The **chest** is deep and of moderate width, having good spring of rib without being barrel shaped.

The **back** is level and strong. The **loin** is short, muscular and slightly arched. The flanks narrow through the loin. The croup is nearly level with the back.

Forequarters and Hindquarters

The front legs are to come straight down from the elbows to the pasterns, whether looking at the dog from the side or the front.

Feet

Feet are very important. Both front and rear feet are round and compact with thick, elastic pads and well-arched toes. Flat feet are a major fault.

Coat and Color Markings

Color and markings and their overall appearance are very important points to be evaluated. The ground color is pure white. In black-spotted dogs the spots are dense black. In liver-spotted dogs the spots are liver brown. Any color markings other than black or liver are disqualified.

Gait

The Dal's gait is peculiar to the breed (and indeed, peculiar within the breed—not all of them are built perfectly enough to do it). The standards of efficiency, endurance and power call for a movement that is *steady and effortless.* The Dal's head position is forward (not erect), held slightly above the topline (at about 9:30 or 10:00 if a clockface reference is used). Her gait at an endurance-paced trot is a smooth, powerful version of a military double-time marching cadence.

Temperament

Temperament is stable and outgoing, yet dignified. Shyness is a major fault.

THE AMERICAN KENNEL CLUB

Familiarly referred to as "the AKC," the American Kennel Club is a nonprofit organization devoted to the advancement of purebred dogs. The AKC maintains a registry of recognized breeds and adopts and enforces rules for dog events including shows, obedience trials, field trials, hunting tests, lure coursing, herding, earth-dog trials, agility and the Canine Good Citizen program. It is a club of clubs, established in 1884 and composed, today, of over 500 autonomous dog clubs throughout the United States. Each club is represented by a delegate; the delegates make up the legislative body of the AKC, voting on rules and electing directors. The American Kennel Club maintains the Stud Book, the record of every dog ever registered with the AKC, and publishes a variety of materials on purebred dogs, including a monthly magazine, books and numerous educational pamphlets. For more information, contact the AKC at the address listed in Chapter 9, "Resources."

A Matter of Fact

The Dalmatian's history has been talked about, written about and guessed at for so long now that nobody really knows the facts. A spotted dog was recorded as early as 3000 B.C. in a colored painting in the Tomb of Redmera at Thebes on the Nile. Subsequently, many other places of origin have been proposed, including Dalmatia (in what used to be southern Yugoslavia, near the Gulf of Venice in the Adriatic Sea), France, Italy, Spain and India. Dals have been referred to in various ways, too, for example: as a Hound, the Spotted Dog of Holland, as a

Pointer, a Great Dane, a Common Harrier, a Bengal Harrier, a Large Bull Terrier, a Bengal Gundog and an Istrian Pointer (which came from crossing mid-European pointers with small harlequin Great Danes). And they've been noted for work as guard dogs, gun dogs, hunters, coaching dogs, entertainers and even pickpockets.

THE DAL DID IT ALL

In some historical observations, the Dal is credited with being a hunting dog, preferring feathered to ground game. We have seen Dals hunt on their own, chasing both ground and feathered game and catching both. Some accounts credit the Dal with being a natural coaching dog, but add that the instinct is not present in all members of the breed (some have no interest and cannot be taught to coach). The remarkable thing about tracing references to the Dal's past is how little hard information exists in comparison to the enormous amount of speculation and logical deduction used to explain their origin.

All things considered, it is prudent to say that spotted dogs have been documented historically, and

In the days before the automobile, horses and carriages needed to be protected and escorted. What better escort than a dog with conspicuous spots?

that spotted dogs have been versatile companions, field dogs and protectors. Regardless of the guesswork as to ancient sightings and specific

FAMOUS OWNERS OF DALMATIANS

George Washington
Pablo Picasso
Gloria Estefan
Melanie Griffith
Don Johnson
Richard Pryor
Paula Abdul
Eugene O'Neill
Richard Simmons

From horse-drawn fire wagons to modern fire engines, the Dalmatian has remained the fireman's mascot.

skills, reports of dogs that clearly resemble what we would recognize as Dalmatians today exist from as early as the mid-seventeenth century. At that time, they were described as coach dogs. Descriptions of Dals as coach dogs in England became common as early as the 1800s.

A First-Class Coach Dog

Judging from their tendencies to work with horses, hunt for game, clear the barn of rats and mice, chase squirrels and birds and catch moles, it's pretty clear that the Dalmatian has parts of his family tree in both the Sporting and Terrier groups of dogs.

Historically, the Dalmatian was probably used for hunting and guarding, and as a palace decoration. The reason he is found in the AKC Non Sporting group is because he has been used to hunt, as a military dog, as a coach dog, a horse barn dog and as a family pet. He may not have the nose (or the need) to compete with the best hounds and he may not "live for retrieving" like a water dog, but the Dal can do both. In addition, the Dal has been a stage performer, is still widely known as the fire station mascot because of his duty with horse-drawn fire wagons, has served in K-9 military duty and as a therapy dog for elderly people. This varied background has produced a dog that today can do nearly anything to the satisfaction of almost any owner.

The Dalmatian's past role was definitely a combination of utility and showpiece, considering his coach dog work and distinctive appearance. Perhaps because of the automobile, which put the coach dog out of a job, his popularity as a unique household pet waned about thirty years ago.

THE IMPACT OF *101 DALMATIANS*

The Walt Disney production of *101 Dalmatians* was released in the 1960s and was an instant success. The public (including children) loved it. The Disney Studios loved it, too, because the animated characters and the story were timeless. Suddenly, Dals were no longer in the barn schmoozing with Nashua. There were relatively steady gains in registrations during the *101 Dalmatians* re-release years, but for the last ten years or so, Dal numbers have been climbing more rapidly. Recent annual AKC figures have shown Dals among the twenty most popular breeds in the country. Considering

It is no wonder why adorable Dalmatian pups were the inspiration for a Walt Disney movie classic.

WHERE DID DOGS COME FROM?

It can be argued that dogs were right there at man's side from the beginning of time. As soon as human beings began to document their existence, the dog was among their drawings and inscriptions. Dogs were not just friends, they served a purpose: There were dogs to hunt birds, pull sleds, herd sheep, burrow after rats—even sit in laps! What your dog was originally bred to do influences the way he behaves. The American Kennel Club recognizes over 140 breeds, and there are hundreds more distinct breeds around the world. To make sense of the breeds, they are grouped according to their size or function. The AKC has seven groups:

1. Sporting
2. Working
3. Herding
4. Hounds
5. Terriers
6. Toys
7. Non Sporting

Can you name a breed from each group? Here's some help: (1) Golden Retriever; (2) Doberman Pinscher; (3) Collie; (4) Beagle; (5) Scottish Terrier; (6) Maltese; and (7) Dalmatian. All modern domestic dogs (*Canis familiaris*) are related, however different they look, and are all descended from *Canis lupus,* the gray wolf.

their rise in popularity, the people in the country who really deserve a gold star are the breeders. Despite the increase in registrations and heightened public interest, breeders have done phenomenal work in improving Dal temperament, health and conformation over the past twenty-five years. It's a phenomenal achievement because increases in popularity and numbers can signal the beginning of the end of quality in a breed. It hasn't happened to Dalmatians, and with proper care and responsible ownership and breeding programs, it doesn't have to.

CHAPTER EIGHT

On Good Behavior

Training is the jewel in the crown— the most important aspect of doggy husbandry. There is no more important variable influencing dog behavior and temperament than the dog's education: A well-trained, well-behaved and good-natured puppydog is always a joy to live with, but an untrained and uncivilized dog can be a perpetual nightmare. Moreover, deny the dog an education and she will not have the opportunity to fulfill her own canine potential; neither will she have the ability to communicate effectively with her human companions.

Luckily, modern psychological training methods are easy, efficient,

OWNING A PARTY ANIMAL

It's a fact: The more of the world your puppy is exposed to, the more comfortable she'll be in it. Once your puppy's had her shots, start taking her everywhere with you. Encourage friendly interaction with strangers, expose her to different environments (towns, fields, beaches) and most important, enroll her in a puppy class where she'll get to play with other puppies. These simple, fun, shared activities will develop your pup into a confident socialite; reliable around other people and dogs.

effective and, above all, considerably dog-friendly and user-friendly. Doggy education is as simple as it is enjoyable. But before you can have a good time play-training with your new dog, you have to learn what to do and how to do it. There is no bigger variable influencing the success of dog training than the owner's experience and expertise. Before you embark on the dog's education, you must first educate yourself.

BASIC TRAINING FOR OWNERS

Ideally, basic owner training should begin well before you select your dog.

Find out all you can about your chosen breed first, then master rudimentary training and handling skills. If you already have your puppydog, owner training is a dire emergency—the clock is ticking! Especially for puppies, the first few weeks at home are the most important and influential days in the dog's life. Indeed, the cause of most adolescent and adult problems may be traced back to the initial days the pup explores her new home. This is the time to establish the *status quo*—to teach the puppydog how you would like her to behave and so prevent otherwise quite predictable problems.

In addition to consulting breeders and breed books such as this one (which understandably have a positive breed bias), seek out as many pet owners with your breed as you can find. Good points are obvious. What you want to find out are the breed-specific problems, so you can nip them in the bud. In particular, you should talk to owners with adolescent dogs and make a list of all anticipated problems. Most important, test drive at least half a dozen adolescent and adult dogs of your breed yourself. An 8-week-old puppy is deceptively easy to handle, but she will acquire adult size, speed and strength in just our months, so you should learn now what to prepare for.

Puppy and pet dog training classes offer a convenient venue to locate pet owners and observe dogs in action. For a list of suitable trainers in your area, contact the Association of Pet Dog Trainers (see chapter 9). You may also begin your basic owner training by observing other owners in class. Watch as many classes and test drive as many dogs as possible. Select an upbeat, dog-friendly, people-friendly, fun-and-games, puppydog pet training class to learn the ropes. Also, watch training videos and read training books. You must find out what to do and how to do it *before* you have to do it.

PRINCIPLES OF TRAINING

Most people think training comprises teaching the dog to do things such as sit, speak and roll over, but even a 4-week-old pup knows how to do these things already. Instead, the first step in training involves teaching the dog human words for each dog behavior and activity and for each aspect of the dog's environment. That way you, the owner, can more easily participate in the dog's

domestic education by directing her to perform specific actions appropriately, that is, at the right time, in the right place and so on. Training opens communication channels, enabling an educated dog to at least understand her owner's requests.

In addition to teaching a dog what we want her to do, it is also necessary to teach her why she should do what we ask. Indeed, 95 percent of training revolves around motivating the dog to want to do what we want. Dogs often understand what their owners want; they just don't see the point of doing it—especially when the owner's repetitively boring and seemingly senseless instructions are totally at odds with much more pressing and exciting doggy distractions. It is not so much the dog that is being stubborn or dominant; rather, it is the owner who has failed to acknowledge the dog's needs and feelings and to approach training from the dog's point of view.

The Meaning of Instructions

The secret to successful training is learning how to use training lures to predict or prompt specific behaviors—to coax the dog to do what you want

61

Knowing what to expect of your puppy prior to her arrival in your home is a great way to stop behavior problems before they start.

when you want. Any highly valued object (such as a treat or toy) may be used as a lure, which the dog will follow with her eyes and nose. Moving the lure in specific ways entices the dog to move her nose, head and entire body in specific ways. In fact, by learning the art of manipulating various lures, it is possible to teach the dog to assume virtually any body position and perform any action. Once you have control over the expression of the dog's behaviors and can elicit any body position or behavior at will, you can easily teach the dog to perform on request.

Tell your dog what you want her to do, use a lure to entice her to

respond correctly, then profusely praise and maybe reward her once she performs the desired action. For example, verbally request "Fido, sit!" while you move a squeaky toy upwards and backwards over the dog's muzzle (lure-movement and hand signal), smile knowingly as she looks up (to follow the lure) and sits down (as a result of canine anatomical engineering), then praise her to distraction ("Gooood Fido!"). Squeak the toy, offer a training treat and give your dog and yourself a pat on the back.

Being able to elicit desired responses over and over enables the owner to reward the dog over and over. Consequently, the dog begins to think training is fun. For example, the more the dog is rewarded for sitting, the more she enjoys sitting. Eventually the dog comes to realize that, whereas most sitting is appreciated, sitting immediately upon request usually prompts especially enthusiastic praise and a slew of high-level rewards. The dog begins to sit on cue much of the time, showing that she is starting to grasp the meaning of the owner's verbal request and hand signal.

Why Comply?

Most dogs enjoy initial lure-reward training and are only too happy to comply with their owners' wishes. Unfortunately, repetitive drilling without appreciative feedback tends to diminish the dog's enthusiasm until she eventually fails to see the point of complying anymore. Moreover, as the dog approaches adolescence she becomes more easily distracted as she develops other interests. Lengthy sessions with repetitive exercises tend to bore and demotivate both parties. If it's not fun, the owner doesn't do it and neither does the dog.

Integrate training into your dog's life: The greater number of training sessions each day and the shorter they are, the more willingly compliant your dog will become. Make sure to have a short (just a few seconds) training interlude before every enjoyable canine activity. For example, ask your dog to sit to greet people, to sit before you throw her Frisbee and to sit for her supper. Really, sitting is no different from a canine "Please." Also, include numerous short training interludes during every enjoyable canine pastime, for example, when playing with the dog or when she is running in the park. In this fashion, doggy distractions may be effectively converted

Food and doggie treats aren't the only lures or rewards that work when training with the lure-reward method; verbal praise or a favorite toy can be just as effective.

Rewarding your Dal when she does something good will aid in teaching her to continue that behavior, such as staying off the couch.

into rewards for training. Just as all games have rules, fun becomes training . . . and training becomes fun.

Eventually, rewards actually become unnecessary to continue motivating your dog. If trained with consideration and kindness, peforming the desired behaviors will become self-rewarding and, in a sense, your dog will motivate herself. Just as it is not necessary to reward a human companion during an enjoyable walk in the park, or following a game of

tennis, it is hardly necessary to reward our best friend—the dog—for walking by our side or while playing fetch. Human company during enjoyable activities is reward enough for most dogs.

Even though your dog has become self-motivating, it's still good to praise and pet her a lot and offer rewards once in a while, especially for a job well done. And if for no other reason, praising and rewarding others is good for the human heart.

Punishment

Without a doubt, lure-reward training is by far the best way to teach: Entice your dog to do what you want and then reward her for doing so. Unfortunately, a human shortcoming is to take the good for granted and to moan and groan at the bad. Specifically, the dog's many good behaviors are ignored while the owner focuses on punishing the dog for making mistakes. In extreme cases, instruction is limited to punishing mistakes made by a trainee dog, child, employee or husband, even though it has been proven punishment training is notoriously inefficient and ineffective and is decidedly unfriendly and combative. It teaches the dog that training is a drag, almost as quickly as it teaches the dog to dislike her trainer. Why treat our best friends like our worst enemies?

Punishment training is also much more laborious and time consuming. Whereas it takes only a finite amount of time to teach a dog what to chew, for example, it takes much, much longer to punish the dog for each and every mistake. Remember, there is only one right way! So why not teach that right way from the outset?!

To make matters worse, punishment training causes severe lapses in the dog's reliability. Since it is obviously impossible to punish the dog each and every time she misbehaves, the dog quickly learns to distinguish between those times when she must comply (so as to avoid impending punishment) and those times when she need not comply, because punishment is impossible. Such times include when the dog is off leash and 6 feet away, when the owner is otherwise engaged (talking to a friend, watching television, taking a shower, tending to the baby or chatting on the telephone) or when the dog is left at home alone.

Instances of misbehavior will be numerous when the owner is away, because even when the dog complied in the owner's looming presence, she did so unwillingly. The dog was forced to act against her will, rather than molding her will to want to please. Hence, when the owner is absent, not only does the dog know she need not comply, she simply does not want to. Again, the trainee is not a stubborn vindictive beast, but rather the trainer has failed to teach. Punishment training invariably creates unpredictable Jekyll and Hyde behavior.

TRAINER'S TOOLS

Many training books extol the virtues of a vast array of training paraphernalia and electronic and metallic gizmos, most of which are designed for canine restraint, correction and punishment, rather than for actual facilitation of doggy education. In reality, most effective training tools are not found in stores; they come from within ourselves. In addition to a willing dog, all you really need is a functional human brain, gentle hands, a loving heart and a good attitude.

In terms of equipment, all dogs do require a quality buckle collar to sport dog tags and to attach the leash (for safety and to comply with local leash laws). Hollow chew toys (like Kongs or sterilized longbones) and a dog bed or collapsible crate are musts for housetraining. Three additional tools are required:

1. specific lures (training treats and toys) to predict and prompt specific desired behaviors;

2. rewards (praise, affection, training treats and toys) to reinforce for the dog what a lot of fun it all is; and

3. knowledge—how to convert the dog's favorite activities and games

After your Dalmatian has relieved herself, reward her by letting her run around and play in a safely enclosed area.

(potential distractions to training) into "life-rewards," which may be employed to facilitate training.

The most powerful of these is knowledge. Education is the key! Watch training classes, participate in training classes, watch videos, read books, enjoy play-training with your dog and then your dog will say "Please," and your dog will say "Thank you!"

HOUSETRAINING

If dogs were left to their own devices, certainly they would chew, dig and bark for entertainment and then no doubt highlight a few areas of their living space with sprinkles of urine, in much the same way we decorate by hanging pictures. Consequently, when we ask a dog to live with us, we must teach her *where* she may dig, *where* she may perform her toilet duties, *what* she may chew and *when* she may bark. After all, when left at home alone for many hours, we cannot expect the dog to amuse herself by completing crosswords or watching TV!

Also, it would be decidedly unfair to keep the house rules a secret from the dog, and then get angry and punish the poor critter for inevitably transgressing rules she did not even know existed. Remember: Without adequate education and guidance, the dog will be forced to establish her own rules—doggy rules—and most probably will be at odds with the owner's view of domestic living.

Since most problems develop during the first few days the dog is at home, prospective dog owners must be certain they are quite clear about the principles of housetraining *before* they get a dog. Early misbehaviors quickly become established as the *status quo*—becoming firmly entrenched

HOUSETRAINING 1-2-3

1. Prevent Mistakes. When you can't supervise your puppy, confine her in a single room or in her crate (but don't leave her for too long!). Puppy-proof the area by laying down newspapers so that if she does make a mistake, it won't matter.

2. Teach Where. Take your puppy to the spot you want her to use every hour.

3. When she goes, praise her profusely and give her three favorite treats.

as hard-to-break bad habits, which set the precedent for years to come. Make sure to teach your dog good habits right from the start. Good habits are just as hard to break as bad ones!

Ideally, when a new dog comes home, try to arrange for someone to be present as much as possible during the first few days (for adult dogs) or weeks for puppies. With only a little forethought, it is surprisingly easy to find a puppy sitter, such as a retired person, who would be willing to eat from your refrigerator and watch your television while keeping an eye on the newcomer to encourage the dog to play with chew toys and to ensure she goes outside on a regular basis.

Potty Training

Follow these steps to teach the dog where she should relieve herself:

1. never let her make a single mistake;

2. let her know where you want her to go; and

3. handsomely reward her for doing so: "GOOOOOOOD DOG!!!" liver treat, liver treat, liver treat!

Preventing Mistakes

A single mistake is a training disaster, since it heralds many more in future weeks. And each time the dog soils the house, this further reinforces the dog's unfortunate preference for an indoor, carpeted toilet. Do not let an unhousetrained dog have full run of the house.

When you are away from home, or cannot pay full attention, confine the dog to an area where elimination is appropriate, such as an outdoor run or, better still, a small, comfortable indoor kennel with access to an outdoor run. When confined in this manner, most dogs will naturally housetrain themselves.

If that's not possible, confine the dog to an area, such as a utility room, kitchen, basement or garage, where elimination may not be desired in the long run but as an interim measure it is certainly preferable to doing it all around the house. Use newspaper to cover the floor of the dog's day room. The newspaper may be used to soak up the urine and to wrap up and dispose of the feces. Once your dog develops a preferred spot for eliminating, it is only necessary to cover that part of the floor with newspaper. The smaller papered area may then be moved (only a little each day) towards the door to the outside. Thus the dog will develop the tendency to go to the door when she needs to relieve herself.

Never confine an unhousetrained dog to a crate for long periods. Doing so would force the dog to soil the crate and ruin its usefulness as an aid for housetraining (see the following discussion).

Teaching Where

In order to teach your dog where you would like her to do her business, you have to be there to direct the proceedings—an obvious, yet often neglected, fact of life. In order to be there to teach the dog where to go, you need to know *when* she needs to go. Indeed, the success of housetraining depends on the owner's ability to predict these times. Certainly, a regular feeding schedule will facilitate prediction somewhat, but there is nothing like "loading the deck" and influencing the timing of the outcome yourself!

Whenever you are at home, make sure the dog is under constant supervision and/or confined to a small area. If already well trained, simply instruct the dog to lie down in her

bed or basket. Alternatively, confine the dog to a crate (doggy den) or tie-down (a short, 18-inch lead that can be clipped to an eye hook in the baseboard near her bed). Short-term close confinement strongly inhibits urination and defecation, since the dog does not want to soil her sleeping area. Thus, when you release the puppydog each hour, she will definitely need to urinate immediately and defecate every third or fourth hour. Keep the dog confined to her doggy den and take her to her intended toilet area each hour, every hour and on the hour. When taking your dog outside, instruct her to sit quietly before opening the door— she will soon learn to sit by the door when she needs to go out!

Teaching Why

Being able to predict when the dog needs to go enables the owner to be on the spot to praise and reward the dog. Each hour, hurry the dog to the intended toilet area in the yard, issue the appropriate instruction ("Go pee!" or "Go poop!"), then give the dog three to four minutes to produce. Praise and offer a couple of training treats when successful. The treats are important because many people fail to praise their dogs with feeling . . . and housetraining is hardly the time for understatement. So either loosen up and enthusiastically praise that dog: "Wuzzer-wuzzer-wuzzer, hoooser good wuffer den? Hoooo went pee for Daddy?" Or say "Good dog!" as best you can and offer the treats for effect.

Following elimination is an ideal time for a spot of play-training in the yard or house. Also, an empty dog may be allowed greater freedom around the house for the next half hour or so, just as long as you keep an eye out to make sure she does not get into other kinds of mischief. If you are preoccupied and cannot pay full attention, confine the dog to her doggy den once more to enjoy a peaceful snooze or to play with her many chew toys.

If your dog does not eliminate within the allotted time outside—no biggie! Back to her doggy den, and then try again after another hour.

As I own large dogs, I always feel more relaxed walking an empty dog, knowing that I will not need to finish our stroll weighted down with bags of feces!

Beware of falling into the trap of walking the dog to get her to eliminate. The good ol' dog walk is such

an enormous highlight in the dog's life that it represents the single biggest potential reward in domestic dogdom. However, when in a hurry, or during inclement weather, many owners abruptly terminate the walk the moment the dog has done her business. This, in effect, severely punishes the dog for doing the right thing, in the right place, at the right time. Consequently, many dogs become strongly inhibited from eliminating outdoors because they know it will signal an abrupt end to an otherwise thoroughly enjoyable walk.

Instead, instruct the dog to relieve herself in the yard prior to going for a walk. If you follow the above instructions, most dogs soon learn to eliminate on cue. As soon as the dog eliminates, praise (and offer a treat or two)—"Good dog! Let's go walkies!" Use the walk as a reward for eliminating in the yard. If the dog does not go, put her back in her doggy den and think about a walk later on. You will find with a "No feces—no walk" policy, your dog will become one of the fastest defecators in the business.

If you do not have a backyard, instruct the dog to eliminate right outside your front door prior to the walk. Not only will this facilitate clean up and disposal of the feces in your own trash can but, also, the walk may again be used as a colossal reward.

CHEWING AND BARKING

Short-term close confinement also teaches the dog that occasional quiet moments are a reality of domestic living. Your puppydog is extremely impressionable during her first few weeks at home. Regular confinement at this time soon exerts a calming influence over the dog's personality. Remember, once the dog is housetrained and calmer, there will be a whole lifetime ahead for the dog to enjoy full run of the

TOYS THAT EARN THEIR KEEP

To entertain even the most distracted of dogs, while you're home or away, have a selection of the following toys on hand: hollow chew toys (like Kongs, sterilized hollow longbones and cubes or balls that can be stuffed with kibble). Smear peanut butter or honey on the inside of the hollow toy or bone and stuff the bone with kibble and your dog will think of nothing else but working the object to get at the food. Great to take your dog's mind off the fact that you've left the house.

house and garden. On the other hand, by letting the newcomer have unrestricted access to the entire

Introducing your puppy to the chew toy will keep her from chewing up your shoes, and will certainly remain your pet's favorite hobby into her adult years.

household and allowing her to run willy-nilly, she will most certainly develop a bunch of behavior problems in short order, no doubt necessitating confinement later in life. It would not be fair to remedially restrain and confine a dog you have trained, through neglect, to run free.

When confining the dog, make sure she always has an impressive array of suitable chew toys. Kongs and sterilized longbones (both readily available from pet stores) make the best chew toys, since they are hollow and may be stuffed with treats to heighten the dog's interest. For example, by stuffing the little hole at the top of a Kong with a small piece of freeze-dried liver, the dog will not want to leave it alone.

Remember, treats do not have to be junk food and they certainly should not represent extra calories. Rather, treats should be part of each dog's regular daily diet: Some food may be served in the dog's bowl for breakfast and dinner, some food may be used as training treats, and some food may be used for stuffing chew toys. I regularly stuff my dogs' many Kongs with different shaped biscuits and kibble. The kibble seems to fall out fairly easily, as do the oval-shaped biscuits, thus rewarding the dog instantaneously for checking out the chew toys. The bone-shaped biscuits fall out after a while, rewarding the dog for worrying at the chew toy. But the triangular biscuits never come out. They remain inside the Kong as lures, maintaining the dog's fascination with her chew toy. To further focus the dog's interest, I always make sure to flavor the triangular biscuits by rubbing them with a little cheese or freeze-dried liver.

If stuffed chew toys are reserved especially for times the dog is confined, the puppydog will soon learn to enjoy quiet moments in her doggy den and she will quickly develop a chew-toy habit—a good habit! This is a simple autoshaping process; all the owner has to do is set up the situation and the dog all but trains herself—easy and effective. Even when the dog is given run of the house, her first inclination will be to indulge her rewarding chew-toy habit rather than destroy less-attractive household articles, such as curtains, carpets, chairs and compact discs. Similarly, a chew-toy chewer will be less inclined to scratch and chew herself excessively. Also, if the dog busies herself as a recreational chewer, she will be

ess inclined to develop into a
recreational barker or digger when
left at home alone.

Stuff a number of chew toys
whenever the dog is left confined
and remove the extra-special-tasting
treats when you return. Your dog
will now amuse herself with her chew
toys before falling asleep and then
resume playing with her chew toys
when she expects you to return.
Since most owner-absent misbehavior happens right after you leave and
right before your expected return,
your puppydog will now be conve-
niently preoccupied with her chew
toys at these times.

COME AND SIT

Most puppies will happily approach
virtually anyone, whether called or
not; that is, until they collide with
adolescence and develop other more
important doggy interests, such as
sniffing a multiplicity of exquisite
odors on the grass. Your mission,
Mr./Ms. Owner, is to teach and reward the pup for coming reliably,
willingly and happily when called—
and you have just three months to
get it done. Unless adequately rein-
forced, your puppy's tendency to approach people will self-destruct by
adolescence.

Call your dog ("Fido, come!"),
open your arms (and maybe squat
down) as a welcoming signal, waggle
a treat or toy as a lure and reward
the puppydog when she comes running. Do not wait to praise the dog
until she reaches you—she may
come 95 percent of the way and

To teach come, call your dog, open your arms as a welcoming signal, wave a toy or a treat and praise for every step in your direction.

then run off after some distraction. Instead, praise the dog's first step towards you and continue praising enthusiastically for every step she takes in your direction.

When the rapidly approaching puppydog is three lengths away from impact, instruct her to sit ("Fido, sit!") and hold the lure in front of you in an outstretched hand to prevent her from hitting you mid-chest and knocking you flat on your back! As Fido decelerates to nose the lure, move the treat upwards and backwards just over her muzzle with an upwards motion of your extended arm (palm-upwards). As the dog looks up to follow the lure, she will sit down (if she jumps up, you are holding the lure too high). Praise the dog for sitting. Move backwards and call her again. Repeat this many times over, always praising when Fido comes and sits; on occasion, reward her.

For the first couple of trials, use a training treat both as a lure to entice the dog to come and sit and as a reward for doing so. Thereafter, try to use different items as lures and rewards. For example, lure the dog with a Kong or Frisbee but reward her with a food treat. Or lure the dog with a food treat but pat her

and throw a tennis ball as a reward. After just a few repetitions, dispense with the lures and rewards; the dog will begin to respond willingly to your verbal requests and hand signals just for the prospect of praise from your heart and affection from your hands.

Instruct every family member, friend and visitor how to get the dog to come and sit. Invite people over for a series of pooch parties; do not keep the pup a secret—let other people enjoy this puppy, and let the pup enjoy other people. Puppydog parties are not only fun, they easily attract a lot of people to help you train your dog. Unless you teach your dog how to meet people, that is, to sit for greetings, no doubt the dog will resort to jumping up. Then you and the visitors will get annoyed, and the dog will be punished. This is not fair. Send out those invitations for puppy parties and teach your dog to be mannerly and socially acceptable.

Even though your dog quickly masters obedient recalls in the house, her reliability may falter when playing in the backyard or local park. Ironically, it is the owner who has unintentionally trained the dog not to respond in these instances. By allowing the dog to play and run around and otherwise have a good time, but then to call the dog to put her on leash to take her home, the dog quickly learns playing is fun but training is a drag. Thus, playing in the park becomes a severe distraction, which works against training. Bad news!

Instead, whether playing with the dog off leash or on leash, request her to come at frequent intervals—say, every minute or so. On most occasions, praise and pet the dog for a few seconds while she is sitting, then tell her to go play again. For especially fast recalls, offer a couple of training treats and take the time to praise and pet the dog enthusiastically before releasing her. The dog will learn that coming when called is not necessarily the end of the play session, and neither is it the end of the world; rather, it signals an enjoyable, quality time-out with the owner before resuming play once more. In fact, playing in the park now becomes a very effective life-reward, which works to facilitate training by reinforcing each obedient and timely recall. Good news!

SIT, DOWN, STAND AND ROLLOVER

Teaching the dog a variety of body positions is easy for owner and dog, impressive for spectators and extremely useful for all. Using lure-reward techniques, it is possible to train several positions at once to verbal commands or hand signals (which impress the socks off onlookers).

Sit and down—the two control commands—prevent or resolve nearly a hundred behavior problems. For example, if the dog happily and obediently sits or lies down when requested, she cannot jump on visitors, dash out the front door, run around and chase her tail, pester other dogs, harass cats or annoy family, friends or strangers. Additionally, "Sit" or "Down" are the best emergency commands for off-leash control.

It is easier to teach and maintain a reliable sit than maintain a reliable recall. Sit is the purest and simplest of commands—either the dog is sitting or she is not. If there is any change of circumstances or potential danger in the park, for example, simply instruct the dog to sit. If she sits, you have a number of options: Allow the dog to resume playing when she is safe, walk up and put the dog on leash or call the dog. The dog will be much more likely to come when called if she has already acknowledged her compliance by sitting. If the dog does not sit in the park—train her to!

Stand and rollover-stay are the two positions for examining the dog. Your veterinarian will love you to distraction if you take a little time to teach the dog to stand still and roll over and play possum. Also, your vet bills will be smaller because it will take the veterinarian less time to examine your dog. The rollover-stay is an especially useful command and is really just a variation of the down-stay: Whereas the dog lies prone in the traditional down, she lies supine in the rollover-stay.

As with teaching come and sit, the training techniques to teach the dog to assume all other body positions on cue are user-friendly and dog-friendly. Simply give the appropriate request, lure the dog into the desired body position using a training treat or toy and then praise (and maybe reward) the dog as soon as she complies. Try not to touch the dog to get her to respond. If you teach the dog by guiding her into position, the dog will quickly learn

that rump-pressure means sit, for example, but as yet you still have no control over your dog if she is just 6 feet away. It will still be necessary to teach the dog to sit on request. So do not make training a time-consuming two-step process; instead, teach the dog to sit to a verbal request or hand signal from the outset. Once the dog sits willingly when requested, by all means use your hands to pet the dog when she does so.

To teach down when the dog is already sitting, say "Fido, down!", hold the lure in one hand (palm down) and lower that hand to the floor between the dog's forepaws. As the dog lowers her head to follow the lure, slowly move the lure away from the dog just a fraction (in front of her paws). The dog will lie down as she stretches her nose forward to follow the lure. Praise the dog when she does so. If the dog stands up, you pulled the lure away too far and too quickly.

When teaching the dog to lie down from the standing position, say "Down" and lower the lure to the floor as before. Once the dog has lowered her forequarters and assumed a play bow, gently and slowly move the lure towards the dog between her forelegs. Praise the dog as soon as her rear end plops down.

After just a couple of trials it will be possible to alternate sits and downs and have the dog energetically perform doggy push-ups. Praise the dog a lot, and after half a dozen or so push-ups reward the dog with a training treat or toy. You will notice the more energetically you move your arm—upwards (palm up) to get the dog to sit, and downwards (palm down) to get the dog to lie down—the more energetically the dog responds to your requests. Now try training the dog in silence and you will notice she has also learned to respond to hand signals. Yeah! Not too shabby for the first session.

To teach stand from the sitting position, say "Fido, stand," slowly move the lure half a dog-length away from the dog's nose, keeping it at nose level, and praise the dog as she stands to follow the lure. As soon as the dog stands, lower the lure to just beneath the dog's chin to entice her to look down; otherwise she will stand and then sit immediately. To prompt the dog to stand from the down position, move the lure half a dog-length upwards and away from the dog, holding the lure at standing nose height from the floor.

Teaching rollover is best started from the down position, with the dog lying on one side, or at least with both hind legs stretched out on the same side. Say "Fido, bang!" and move the lure backwards and alongside the dog's muzzle to her elbow (on the side of her outstretched hind legs). Once the dog looks to the side and backwards, very slowly move the lure upwards to the dog's shoulder and backbone. Tickling the dog in the goolies (groin area) often invokes a reflex-raising of the hind leg as an appeasement gesture, which facilitates the tendency to roll over. If you move the lure too quickly and the dog jumps into the standing position, have patience and start again. As soon as the dog rolls onto her back, keep the lure stationary and mesmerize the dog with a relaxing tummy rub.

To teach rollover-stay when the dog is standing or moving, say "Fido, bang!" and give the appropriate hand signal (with index finger pointed and thumb cocked in true Sam Spade fashion), then in one fluid movement lure her to first lie down and then rollover-stay as above.

Teaching the dog to stay in each of the above four positions becomes a piece of cake after first teaching

FINDING A TRAINER

Have fun with your dog, take a training class! But don't just sign on any dotted line, find a trainer whose approach and style you like and whose students (and their dogs) are really learning. Ask to visit a class to observe a trainer in action. For the names of trainers near you, ask your veterinarian, your pet supply store, your dog-owning neighbors or call (800) PET-DOGS (the Association of Pet Dog Trainers).

the dog not to worry at the toy or treat training lure. This is best accomplished by hand feeding dinner kibble. Hold a piece of kibble firmly in your hand and softly instruct "Off!" Ignore any licking and slobbering for however long the dog worries at the treat, but say "Take it!" and offer the kibble the instant the dog breaks contact with her muzzle. Repeat this a few times, and then up the ante and insist the dog remove her muzzle for one whole second before offering the kibble. Then progressively refine your criteria and have the dog not touch your hand (or treat) for longer and longer periods on each trial, such as for two seconds, four seconds, then six, ten, fifteen, twenty, thirty seconds and so on.

The dog soon learns: (1) worrying at the treat never gets results, whereas (2) noncontact is often rewarded after a variable time lapse.

Teaching "Off!" has many useful applications in its own right. Additionally, instructing the dog not to touch a training lure often produces spontaneous and magical stays. Request the dog to stand-stay, for example, and not to touch the lure. At first set your sights on a short two-second stay before rewarding the dog. (Remember, every long journey begins with a single step.) However, on subsequent trials, gradually and progressively increase the length of stay required to receive a reward. In no time at all your dog will stand calmly for a minute or so.

RELEVANCY TRAINING

Once you have taught the dog what you expect her to do when requested to come, sit, lie down, stand, rollover and stay, the time is right to teach the dog why she should comply with your wishes. The secret is to have many (many) extremely short training interludes (two to five seconds each) at numerous (numerous) times during the course of the dog's day.

Especially work with the dog immediately before the dog's good times and during the dog's good times. For example, ask your dog to sit and/or lie down each time before opening doors, serving meals, offering treats and tummy rubs; ask the dog to perform a few controlled doggy push-ups before letting her off leash or throwing a tennis ball; and perhaps request the dog to sit-down-sit-stand-down-stand-rollover before inviting her to cuddle on the couch.

Similarly, request the dog to sit many times during play or on walks, and in no time at all the dog will be only too pleased to follow your instructions because she has learned that a compliant response heralds all sorts of goodies. Basically all you are trying to teach the dog is how to say please: "Please throw the tennis ball. Please may I snuggle on the couch."

Remember, it is important to keep training interludes short and to have many short sessions each and every day. The shortest (and most useful) session comprises asking the dog to sit and then go play during a play session. When trained this way, your dog will soon associate training with good times. In fact, the dog may be unable to distinguish between training and good times and, indeed, there should be no distinction. The warped concept that training involves forcing the dog to comply and/or dominating her will is totally at odds with the picture of a truly well-trained dog. In reality, enjoying a game of training with a dog is no different from enjoying a game of backgammon or tennis with a friend; and walking with a dog should be no different from strolling with a spouse, or with buddies on the golf course.

WALK BY YOUR SIDE

Many people attempt to teach a dog to heel by putting her on a leash and physically correcting the dog when she makes mistakes. There are a number of things seriously wrong with this approach, the first being that most people do not want precision heeling; rather, they simply want the dog to follow or walk by their side. Second, when physically restrained during "training," even though the dog may grudgingly mope by your side when "handcuffed" on leash, let's see what happens when she is off leash. History! The dog is in the next county because she never enjoyed

Using a food lure to teach "Sit," "Down" and "Stand."

1) "Phoenix, Sit."

2) Hand palm upwards, move lure up and back over dog's muzzle.

3) "Good sit, Phoenix!"

4) "Phoenix, Down."

5) Hand palm downwards, move lure down to lie between dog's forepaws.

6) "Phoenix, Off. Good down, Phoenix!"

80

7) "Phoenix, Sit!"

8) Palm upwards, move lure up and back, keeping it close to dog's muzzle.

9) "Good sit, Phoenix!"

10) *"Phoenix, Stand!"*
11) *Move lure away from dog at nose height, then lower it a tad.*
12) *"Phoenix, Off! Good stand, Phoenix!"*

13) *"Phoenix, Down!"*
14) *Hand palm downwards, move lure down to lie between dog's forepaws.*
15) *"Phoenix, Off! Good down-stay, Phoenix!"*

81

16) *"Phoenix, Stand!"*
17) *Move lure away from dog's muzzle up to nose height.*
18) *"Phoenix, Off! Good stand-stay, Phoenix."*

walking with you on leash and you have no control over her off leash. So let's just teach the dog off leash from the outset to want to walk with us. Third, if the dog has not been trained to heel, it is a trifle hasty to think about punishing the poor dog for making mistakes and breaking heeling rules she didn't even know existed. This is simply not fair! Surely, if the dog had been adequately taught how to heel, she would seldom make mistakes and hence there would be no need to correct the dog. Remember, each mistake and each correction (punishment) advertise the trainer's inadequacy, not the dog's. The dog is not stubborn, she is not stupid and she is not bad. Even if she were, she would still require training, so let's train her properly.

Let's teach the dog to enjoy following us and to want to walk by our side off leash. Then it will be easier to teach high-precision off-leash heeling patterns if desired. Before going on outdoor walks, it is necessary to teach the dog not to pull. Then it becomes easy to teach on-leash walking and heeling because the dog already wants to walk with you, she is familiar with the desired walking and heeling positions and she knows not to pull.

FOLLOWING

Start by training your dog to follow you. Many puppies will follow if you simply walk away from them and maybe click your fingers or chuckle. Adult dogs may require additional enticement to stimulate them to follow, such as a training lure or, at the very least, a lively trainer. To teach the dog to follow: (1) keep walking and (2) walk away from the dog. If the dog attempts to lead or lag, change pace; slow down if the dog forges too far ahead, but speed up if she lags too far behind. Say "Steady!" or "Easy!" each time before you slow down and "Quickly!" or "Hustle!" each time before you speed up, and the dog will learn to change pace on cue. If the dog lags or leads too far, or if she wanders right or left, simply walk quickly in the opposite direction and maybe even run away from the dog and hide.

Practicing is a lot of fun; you can set up a course in your home, yard or park to do this. Indoors, entice the dog to follow upstairs, into a bedroom, into the bathroom, downstairs, around the living room couch, zigzagging between dining room chairs and into the kitchen for dinner. Outdoors, get the dog to follow around park benches, trees, shrubs and along walkways and lines in the grass. (For safety outdoors, it is advisable to attach a long line on the dog, but never exert corrective tension on the line.)

Remember, following has a lot to do with attitude—your attitude! Most probably your dog will not want to follow Mr. Grumpy Troll with the personality of wilted lettuce. Lighten up—walk with a jaunty step, whistle a happy tune, sing, skip and tell jokes to your dog and she will be right there by your side.

BY YOUR SIDE

It is smart to train the dog to walk close on one side or the other— either side will do, your choice. When walking, jogging or cycling, it is generally bad news to have the dog suddenly cut in front of you. In fact, I train my dogs to walk "By my side" and "Other side"—both very useful instructions. It is possible to position the dog fairly accurately by looking to the appropriate side and clicking your fingers or slapping your thigh on that side. A pre-

cise positioning may be attained by holding a training lure, such as a chew toy, tennis ball, or food treat. Stop and stand still several times throughout the walk, just as you would when window shopping or meeting a friend. Use the lure to make sure the dog slows down and stays close whenever you stop.

When teaching the dog to heel, we generally want her to sit in heel position when we stop. Teach heel position at the standstill and the dog will learn that the default heel position is sitting by your side (left or right—your choice, unless you wish to compete in obedience trials, in which case the dog must heel on the left).

Several times a day, stand up and call your dog to come and sit in heel position—"Fido, heel!" For example, instruct the dog to come to heel each time there are commercials on TV, or each time you turn a page of a novel, and the dog will get it in a single evening.

Practice straight-line heeling and turns separately. With the dog sitting at heel, teach her to turn in place. After each quarter-turn, half-turn or full turn in place, lure the dog to sit at heel. Now it's time for short straight-line heeling sequences, no more than a few steps at a time. Always think of heeling in terms of sit-heel-sit sequences—start and end with the dog in position and do your best to keep her there when moving. Progressively increase the number of steps in each sequence. When the dog remains close for 20 yards of straight-line heeling, it is time to add a few turns and then sign up for a happy-heeling obedience class to get some advice from the experts.

No Pulling on Leash

You can start teaching your dog not to pull on leash anywhere—in front of the television or outdoors—but regardless of location, you must not take a single step with tension in the leash. For a reason known only to dogs, even just a couple of paces of pulling on leash is intrinsically motivating and diabolically rewarding. Instead, attach the leash to the dog's collar, grasp the other end firmly with both hands held close to your chest, and stand still—do not budge an inch. Have somebody watch you with a stopwatch to time your progress, or else you will never believe this will work and so you will

not even try the exercise, and your shoulder and the dog's neck will be traumatized for years to come.

Stand still and wait for the dog to stop pulling, and to sit and/or lie down. All dogs stop pulling and sit eventually. Most take only a couple of minutes; the all-time record is $22\frac{1}{2}$ minutes. Time how long it takes. Gently praise the dog when she stops pulling, and as soon as she sits, enthusiastically praise the dog and take just one step forward, then immediately stand still. This single step usually demonstrates the ballistic reinforcing nature of pulling on leash; most dogs explode to the end of the leash, so be prepared for the strain. Stand firm and wait for the dog to sit again. Repeat this half a dozen times and you will probably notice a progressive reduction in the force of the dog's one-step explosions and a radical reduction in the time it takes for the dog to sit each time.

As the dog learns "Sit we go" and "Pull we stop," she will begin to walk forward calmly with each single step and automatically sit when you stop. Now try two steps before you stop. Wooooooo! Scary! When the dog has mastered two steps at a time, try for three. After each success, progressively increase the number of steps in the sequence: try four steps and then six, eight, ten and twenty steps before stopping. Congratulations! You are now walk-ing the dog on leash.

Whenever walking with the dog (off leash or on leash), make sure you stop periodically to practice a few position commands and stays before instructing the dog to "Walk on!"

Integrating training into a walk offers 200 separate opportunities to use the continuance of the walk as a reward to reinforce the dog's education.

CHAPTER NINE

Resources

BOOKS

About Dalmatians

Ackerman, Lowell J. *Dr. Ackerman's Book of the Dalmatian.* Neptune, NJ: Tfh Publications, 1996.

Dalmatian Club of America. *The Official Book of the Dalmatian.* Neptune, NJ: Tfh Publications, 1997.

Silverstone, Patches. *Dalmatians Today.* New York: Howell Book House, 1997.

Treen, Alfred, and Esmerelda Treen. *The New Dalmatian.* New York: Howell Book House, 1992.

About Health Care

American Kennel Club. *American Kennel Club Dog Care and Training.* New York: Howell Book House, 1991.

Carlson, Delbert, DVM, and James Giffen, MD. *Dog Owner's Home Veterinary Handbook.* New York: Howell Book House, 1992.

DeBitetto, James, DVM, and Sarah Hodgson. *You & Your Puppy.* New York: Howell Book House, 1995.

Lane, Marion. *The Humane Society of the United States Complete Guide to Dog Care.* New York: Little, Brown & Co., 1998.

McGinnis, Terri. *The Well Dog Book.* New York: Random House, 1991.

Schwartz, Stephanie, DVM. *First Aid for Dogs: An Owner's Guide to a Happy Healthy Pet.* New York: Howell Book House, 1998.

Volhard, Wendy and Kerry L. Brown. *The Holistic Guide for a Healthy Dog.* New York: Howell Book House, 1995.

About Training

Ammen, Amy. *Training in No Time.* New York: Howell Book House, 1995.

Benjamin, Carol Lea. *Mother Knows Best.* New York: Howell Book House, 1985.

Bohnenkamp, Gwen. *Manners for the Modern Dog.* San Francisco: Perfect Paws, 1990.

Dunbar, Ian, Ph.D., MRCVS. *Dr. Dunbar's Good Little Book.* James & Kenneth Publishers, 2140 Shattuck Ave. #2406, Berkeley, CA 94704. (510) 658-8588. Order from Publisher.

Evans, Job Michael. *People, Pooches and Problems.* New York: Howell Book House, 1991.

Palika, Liz. *All Dogs Need Some Training.* New York: Howell Book House, 1997.

Volhard, Jack and Melissa Bartlett. *What All Good Dogs Should Know: The Sensible Way to Train.* New York: Howell Book House, 1991.

About Activities

Hall, Lynn. *Dog Showing for Beginners.* New York: Howell Book House, 1994.

O'Neil, Jackie. *All About Agility.* New York: Howell Book House, 1998.

Simmons-Moake, Jane. *Agility Training, The Fun Sport for All Dogs.* New York: Howell Book House, 1991.

Vanacore, Connie. *Dog Showing: An Owner's Guide.* New York: Howell Book House, 1990.

Volhard, Jack and Wendy. *The Canine Good Citizen.* New York: Howell Book House, 1994.

MAGAZINES

THE AKC GAZETTE, The Official Journal for the Sport of Purebred Dogs
American Kennel Club
260 Madison Ave.
New York, NY 10016
www.akc.org

DOG FANCY
Fancy Publications
3 Burroughs
Irvine, CA 92618
(714) 855-8822
http://dogfancy.com

DOG WORLD
Maclean Hunter Publishing Corp.
500 N. Dearborn, Ste. 1100
Chicago, IL 60610
(312) 396-0600
www.dogworldmag.com

PETLIFE: YOUR COMPANION ANIMAL MAGAZINE
Magnolia Media Group
1400 Two Tandy Center
Fort Worth, TX 76102
(800) 767-9377
www.petlifeweb.com

DOG & KENNEL
7-L Dundas Circle
Greensboro, NC 27407
(336) 292-4047
www.dogandkennel.com

87

MORE INFORMATION ABOUT DALMATIANS

National Breed Club

DALMATIAN CLUB OF
AMERICA, INC.
Corresponding Secretary:
  Sharon Boyd
  2316 McCrary Rd.
  Richmond, TX 77469
Breeder Contact:
  Gerri Lightholder
  6109 W. 147th St.
  Oak Forest, IL 60452
  (708) 687-5447
Breed Rescue:
  Chris Jackson
  (410) 902-9044

The Club can send you information on all aspects of the breed including the names and addresses of breed clubs in your area, as well as obedience clubs. Inquire about membership.

The American Kennel Club

The American Kennel Club (AKC), devoted to the advancement of purebred dogs, is the oldest and largest registry organization in this country. Every breed recognized by the AKC has a national (parent) club. National clubs are a great source of information on your breed. The affiliated clubs hold AKC events and use AKC rules to hold performance events, dog shows, educational programs, health clinics and training classes. The AKC staff is divided between offices in New

York City and Raleigh, North Carolina. The AKC has an excellent Web site that provides information on the organization and all AKC-recognized breeds. The address is www.akc.org.

For registration and performance events information, or for customer service, contact:

THE AMERICAN KENNEL CLUB
5580 Centerview Dr., Suite 200
Raleigh, NC 27606
(919) 233-9767
The AKC's executive offices and the AKC Library (open to the public) are at this address:

THE AMERICAN KENNEL CLUB
260 Madison Ave.
New York, New York 10016
(212) 696-8200 (general information)
(212) 696-8246 (AKC Library)
www.akc.org

UNITED KENNEL CLUB
100 E. Kilgore Rd.
Kalamazoo, MI 49001-5598
(616) 343-9020
www.ukcdogs.com

AMERICAN RARE BREED
ASSOCIATION
9921 Frank Tippett Rd.
Cheltenham, MD 20623
(301) 868-5718 (voice or fax)
www.arba.org

CANADIAN KENNEL CLUB
89 Skyway Ave., Ste. 100
Etobicoke, Ontario
Canada M9W 6R4
(416) 675-5511
www.ckc.ca

ORTHOPEDIC FOUNDATION
FOR ANIMALS (OFA)
2300 E. Nifong Blvd.
Columbia, MO 65201-3856
(314) 442-0418
www.offa.org/

Trainers

Animal Behavior & Training
Associates (ABTA)
9018 Balboa Blvd., Ste. 591
Northridge, CA 91325
(800) 795-3294
www.Good-dawg.com

Association of Pet Dog Trainers
(APDT)
(800) PET-DOGS
www.apdt.com

National Association of Dog
Obedience Instructors (NADOI)
729 Grapevine Highway, Ste. 369
Hurst, TX 76054-2085
www.kimberly.uidaho.edu/nadoi

Associations

Delta Society
P.O. Box 1080
Renton, WA 98507-1080

(Promotes the human/animal bond
through pet-assisted therapy and other
programs)
www.petsforum.com/
DELTASOCIETY/dsi400.htm

Dog Writers Association of
America (DWAA)
Sally Cooper, Secretary
222 Woodchuck Lane
Harwinton, CT 06791
www.dwaa.org

National Association for Search
and Rescue (NASAR)
4500 Southgate Place, Ste. 100
Chantilly, VA 20157
(703) 222-6277
www.nasar.org

Therapy Dogs International
6 Hilltop Rd.
Mendham, NJ 07945

OTHER USEFUL RESOURCES— WEB SITES

General Information— Links to Additional Sites, On-Line Shopping

www.k9web.com – resources for the dog
world

www.netpet.com – pet related products,
software and services

www.apapets.com – The American Pet
Association

www.dogandcatbooks.com – book
catalog

www.dogbooks.com – on-line bookshop

www.animal.discovery.com/ – cable
television channel on-line

Health

www.avma.org – American Veterinary
Medical Association (AVMA)

www.aplb.org – Association for Pet Loss
Bereavement (APLB)—contains an

89

index of national hot lines for on-line and office counseling.

www.netfopets.com/AskTheExperts. html – veterinary questions answered on-line.

Breed Information

www.bestdogs.com/news/ – newsgroup

www.cheta.net/connect/canine/breeds/ – Canine Connections Breed Information Index

Kennel cough, 27, 32
Kidney stones, 35

Leashes, 10, 13, 84-85
Lice, 31
Limping, 33
Lumps, 33
Lure-reward training, 5-6, 13, 61-63, 66-67
Lyme disease, 26-27, 31

Mange, 31
Markings, 49, 52-53
Mites, 31
Motivation during training, 61, 64

Nails, 41-43
Neutering, 22-23
Nose, 52
Nutrition. *See* Food

Obesity, 34
Off command, 78, 81
Outdoor confinement, 13

Parasites, 29-31
Parvovirus, 24-25
Pecking order, 7, 9-11
Personality
    during homecoming, 8-9
    hyperactive, 6
    intelligence, 3, 45-46
    pecking order, 7, 9-11
    puppies, 9
    shyness, 7, 10
    socialization, 1, 6, 9, 19, 24, 60, 74
    "smiling," 4
    temperament, 1-3, 47, 53
Play-training, 63, 70, 75, 78-79

Poisonous substances, 14-16, 28
Popularity, 57-58
Positive reinforcement, 12
Preventive health care, 17, 21-22, 31
Price range for puppies, 11-12
Protein, 35
Punishment, 65-66
Puppies
    food, 34-35
    personality, 9
    proofing your home, 8-9
    training, 60-61
Purine, 17-19, 35
Pyometra, 22

Rabies, 24
Rocky Mountain Spotted Fever, 31
Rollover command 76-78
Roundworms (ascarids), 20
Runny nose, 32

Shyness, 7, 10
Sit command, 73-78, 80
Size, 50
Skin allergies, 19-20
Sleeping quarters, 14
"smiling," 5
Socialization, 1, 6-7, 9, 19, 24, 60, 74
Spaying, 22-23
Split ears/tails, 20-21
Stand/stay command, 76-78, 80-81
Strength, 50

Tails, split, 20-21
Tapeworms, 29
Teeth, 33, 44
Ticks, 30-31

Toys, chewing, 10, 13, 15-16, 66, 72
Training
    barking, 6, 71-73
    chewing, 15-16, 71-73
    classes, 61, 78
    come and sit command, 73-75
    communication, 61
    developing bad habits, 4, 59, 72
    heel command, 79, 82-83
    housetraining, 13-15, 67-68
    jumping, 4
    leashes, 13, 84-85
    lure-reward, 5-6, 13, 61-63, 66-67
    motivation, 61, 64
    off command, 78, 81
    owners, 60-61
    play-training, 63, 70, 75, 78-79
    positive reinforcement, 12
    potty training, 68-71
    praising, 64
    punishment, 65-66
    sit, down, stand and rollover command, 75-78, 80-81
    walking, 79, 82-85
treats/biscuits, 16, 38, 66, 71

Vaccinations, 23, 25, 27
Veterinarians, 23, 27
Vitamin supplements, 36
Vomiting/retching, 32

Walking, 70, 79, 82-85
Water, 10, 13
Weight, 48
Whipworms, 30
Whiskers, 44-45

Put a picture of your dog
in this box

Your Dog's Name ....

Your Dog's License Number _____

Date of Birth _____

Your Dog's Veterinarian _____

Address _____

Phone Number _____

Medications _____

Vet Emergency Number _____

Additional Emergency Numbers _____

Feeding Instructions _____

Exercise Routine _____

Favorite Treats _____

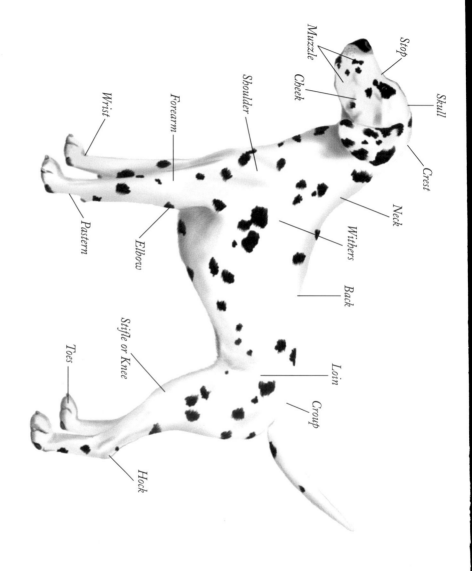

Dalmatian

Muzzle

Stop

Cheek

Skull

Shoulder

Crest

Wrist

Forearm

Neck

Withers

Pastern

Elbow

Back

Stifle or Knee

Loin

Toes

Croup

Hock